SELF-MASTERY THROUGH THE TWELVE RAYS

Twelve Keys to Self-Realization

Janet Houser

Writers Club Press
San Jose New York Lincoln Shanghai

SELF-MASTERY THROUGH THE TWELVE RAYS
Twelve Keys to Self-Realization

Writers Club Press
an imprint of iUniverse.com, Inc.

For information address:
iUniverse.com, Inc.
5220 S 16th, Ste. 200
Lincoln, NE 68512
www.iuniverse.com

ISBN: 0-595-19318-8

Printed in the United States of America

Contents

Preface

"I have already given you more than you can understand, but not more than you can slowly begin to study and eventually to comprehend."

(6-366)

From Master Djwhal Khul.
Serving Humanity[1]

The study of the original *A Treatise on the Seven Rays*[2] is a challenge. Certainly, even the most articulate advanced minds of vast education and gifted intelligence will find themselves scratching their heads in wonderment of what the pages are saying. Because the great works of Alice A. Bailey and the Tibetan Master Djwhal Khul are of such a profound nature and written with such deep understanding of a subject that we can only slightly begin to comprehend, it is often very difficult for even the most ambitious readers to follow, perceive, and remember. **It is my intention to present the Twelve Rays in a basic way**. Simplifying this information is like teaching a triple Ph.D. program at the elementary school level. I am gathering a small compilation of what I feel is the "heart" of the Twelve Rays, and I humbly offer it to humanity with the hope of opening up minds and making the knowledge available to us all at a level that we can understand. In this spirit of service and humility, I give you this book. I encourage you to read the original works of Alice A. Bailey and the Tibetan Master Djwhal Khul as you are guided to do so personally.

Self-Mastery Through the Twelve Rays is a product of my study of Theosophy, the Alice A. Bailey books, private study with a spiritual teacher, my notes of her teachings, and channeled direction from God. Even though this material is a very simple introduction of the Twelve Rays, it is intensely valuable in our understanding of our lives, our personal development, and our spiritual advancement.

I wish to make the Twelve Rays *real* to you. I want you to be able to understand the rays and *use* them in your lives.

Journey to Self-Empowerment

The study and application of the twelve rays is empowering. It is an honor for me to participate in your journey to self-empowerment. Since this is *your journey*, I will be functioning as your guide and facilitator. Together we will help unlock the secrets of the universe located within you. Discovering the universal truths and learning how to channel the power of the universe into constructive use in your own life is our mutual goal for you.

This book is about living your life with **intentionality**. The processes that I will be leading you through will help you to discover your own truth. This work is not about religion or philosophy or imposition of one set of values over another. It is about **honoring the soul**. By showing you how to go within yourself, I will show you how to locate your true nature, discover who you really are, determine your goals in life, and how to become **your authentic self**.

People of all religious, philosophical, and cultural backgrounds can participate in this journey successfully if they believe in the sacredness of life and the freedom of the individual. Actually, that is what this learning is about—honoring life, finding the sacredness in ordinary life, and embracing your own free will with purpose. This journey is about releasing the fears, limitations, and stored stresses that every person harbors within. Regardless of your race, religion, occupation, sex, station in life, level of education, you are basically being held back from becoming your best because of these very things—*fear and limitation, lack of self-knowledge,* stuck energy, and stored stresses. *The knowledge and application of the twelve rays is one of the most powerful tools available to humanity.*

In over thirty years of vast study, I have learned many tools in how to empower people. I am combining the results of a variety of studies to bring to you a rewarding journey of self-empowerment. I look forward to sharing my wisdom and expertise with you.

From the human perspective, it is not possible for us to know everything in the universe, but we can learn how to live with the mystery and to honor our souls.

Acknowledgments

To Emmabelle

I am deeply grateful to the following authors whose works I have consulted in my study of the Twelve Rays: Alice A. Bailey (who was the channel for the Ascended Master Djwhal Khul), Annie Besant, H.P. Blavatsky, Helen Burmester, Brian Grattan, Ronna Herman, Zachary Lansdowne, Janet McClure, Dr. Joshua David Stone, and Ernest Wood.

Many wonderful people have been great sources of inspiration and encouragement in my writing of this book. I would like to especially thank my friends Bill Deeg, Jane Root, Luckie Bosselman, Robert Eckhardt, and my pilot group (who were the first students to study this material with me): Deborah Caine, Patti Deeg, Sandy Herbstman, Rachel Johnston, Patti Levine, Ricki Stewart, Fred Tippins, Phyllis Trammel, and Jeanne Ward. Thank you all for being the "wind beneath my wings."

I especially wish to thank the ascended masters who have helped me with the writing of this book: Djwhal Khul, Lord Maitreya, Kuthumi, Archangel Michael, and other great beings of Light. I am humbly grateful for their inspiration and connection to me. I dedicate this book to all of the great teachers in my life, my special Seven Rays teacher Emmabelle Donath, my wonderful family, dear friends, and every special soul who has helped me to become who I am today and has contributed to the manifestation of this book.

Introduction

This book has been ten years in the making. In 1991, I was a college instructor, an avid student of metaphysics and seeker of spiritual truths. Emmabelle Donath, an astrologer and spiritual teacher, invited me to study a course that she was teaching called "The Seven Rays." Although I had no idea what "The Seven Rays" meant, I was intrigued by the title and joined the small group of selected students who met in her home over a period of several months.

I learned that The Seven Rays are energies radiated to our planet from the Undifferentiated Source of all life and that these energies affect all life on every level. The Seven Rays information contained in this book comes from the Alice A. Bailey written works on Theosophy, which is the synthesis of Science, Religion, and Philosophy, as well as more recent written works.

At the time of the classes, I took copious notes. There were times when Emmabelle said, "This is not written down anywhere, so be sure to take notes!" I did just that. I believe that the information on the characteristics of the physical bodies was channeled through Emmabelle. The rest of the material can be documented in the works of Alice A. Bailey.

During the course of my studies with Emmabelle in 1991, she took me aside one evening and said to me, "Some day you will teach this." Because I was a college instructor at the time, teaching was not a big "stretch" for me. The material, however, was new and profound to me, and I really could not imagine that I would be qualified to relay this in the wonderful way that Emmabelle had done. She was so fluent in the sacred knowledge of the universe that it seemed as if she had a direct pipeline to the higher truths. I am convinced that she did. Seeing myself teaching the Seven Rays with her expertise and wisdom seemed impossible to me then.

Sadly, Emmabelle passed away at age 61 from cancer. She departed during the time that we were still studying with her, and it was a great loss for us all. On more than one occasion, Emmabelle told us that it was not important who she was or what rank she held spiritually. All that mattered was the information that she was imparting to us. I have since read that statement in Alice A. Bailey's books and admire Emmabelle for her humility and purity. Even at her deathbed, she demonstrated this simplicity. When Charlotte, one of the students, said, "I will never forget you, Emmabelle, for you have taught me so much," Emmabelle replied, "It doesn't matter where you learned it. All that matters is you learned it."

I wish that Emmabelle were still here because of my great love and respect for her; I also wish I could ask her some questions and discuss this book with her. I have felt her spiritual presence very often since she passed away, and I have felt directed by her to write this book. She has been a spiritual guide to me, and I cherish this honor.

After Emmabelle's death, I treasured my notes from The Seven Rays classes even more. Every few months, I would read them and wonder if her prophecy that I would teach The Seven Rays was true. I felt incomplete in my knowledge and alone in my awareness that The Seven Rays even existed. It seemed that there was not enough written material to rely on as a resource for the average student. The Alice A. Bailey books that I was reading: *Discipleship in the New Age, The Rays and the Initiations, Esoteric Healing, Esoteric Psychology*, etc., were fascinating to me, but also overwhelming. A few times I cautiously mentioned the fact that I had studied The Seven Rays to friends, who surprised me by responding with great interest and encouragement to teach this in a class. I waited for guidance and a sign from God.

The sign came in 1999. One day while I was reading the *Sedona Journal of Emergence,*[3] I noticed an advertisement for the "I AM Mastery Course," channeled by Archangel Michael through Ronna Herman.[4] My split-second reaction was to order this written course with no hesitation. I was simply compelled to do it! I had no idea why I was so instantly attracted to it. There were many spiritual classes being advertised that I had not responded to, and I am not an impulsive person. When the written course and audiotapes arrived, I saw the title, "The Seven Rays." A chill went through me. This was it! My sign from God had arrived! I knew that it was time for me to teach The Seven Rays. I plunged into studying the "I AM Mastery" course and organizing it for teaching purposes like a starving woman who had just been presented with a feast. At that moment, an invisible "force" took over that has directed me ever since.

Since that day, I have been guided by angels and beings of great majesty while writing the Seven Rays Course, which I added to the "I AM Mastery" Course, and this book *Self-Mastery Through the Twelve Rays.* For this heavenly opportunity, I thank the ascended master Djwhal Khul, Archangel Michael, Emmabelle Donath, Ronna Herman, the great cosmic beings of Light, and the grace of God.

Janet Houser
June 2001

Part One

Chapter 1

What Are the Twelve Rays?

The Twelve Rays are basic energies. They comprise the frequency bands of electrical energy coming into the earth. This electrical energy is radiated out from the Undifferentiated Source to the whole world, planets, everything in existence. In volume 1 of *Esoteric Psychology (p. 316)*, Alice Bailey defines a "ray" in the following way:

> *"A ray is but a name for a particular force or type of energy with the emphasis upon the quality which that force exhibits and not upon the form aspect which it creates." This is a true definition of a ray.'*

There are many different rays in existence. Prior to 1991, only seven rays could touch our planet. On January 26, 1991, five higher rays became anchored into the Earth, and we now have twelve rays available to help us ascend into higher consciousness. Since the five higher rays are various blends of The Seven Rays infused with higher Light, the major focus of this book will be on The Seven Rays, with a brief discussion of all twelve rays and their significance.

Each of The Twelve Rays represents attributes and characteristics of the Creator. (We will be learning about these specific qualities in greater detail in later chapters). There are three groups of rays. Rays One, Two and Three are called *Rays of Aspect*. They are the primary rays for the purpose of creating, and they are self-satisfying. Rays Four, Five, Six and Seven are called *Rays of Attribute*. These rays are for the purpose of providing experiences and are considered to be auxiliary rays. Rays Eight, Nine, Ten, Eleven and Twelve are called the *Higher Rays* and are *blends* of the other Seven Rays infused with Christ Light. Very briefly described, the qualities of The Seven Rays are as follows:

Ray One: Divine Will and Power
Ray Two: Love and Wisdom
Ray Three: Active Intelligence
Ray Four: Harmony Through Conflict
Ray Five: Concrete Knowledge and Science
Ray Six: Devotion, Adoration and Idealism
Ray Seven: Ceremonial Magic and Order

Each ray has higher and lower aspects. When we have absorbed *all* of the highest aspects and attributes of the Seven Rays into our own essence, we achieve self-mastery. Each of the Seven Rays has a color as well as attributes and aspects. The rainbow with its seven colors is symbolic of the Seven Rays. Each ray corresponds to a specific color of the rainbow; for example:

Ray One = Red
Ray Two = Blue
Ray Three = Yellow
Ray Four = Green
Ray Five = Orange
Ray Six = Indigo
Ray Seven = Violet

Chapter 2

The Difference Between Rays and Chakras

The Seven Rays differ from the seven chakras (spinning wheels of energy in the human body). The chakras are energy centers within the etheric body. The Seven Rays are energies radiated to our planet from the Undifferentiated Source of all life. The Seven Rays impact the chakra system, and each ray has a special impact on a specific chakra. However, *rays and chakras are not interchangeable terms.*

Chapter 3

Why Study the Twelve Rays?

Studying the Twelve Rays is a powerful method of learning your soul's purpose, your divine mission, your strengths and weaknesses, how you relate to others, the path you take in life, how to live your life to your highest potential, and how to heal yourself. We call this branch of study "Esoteric (Spiritual) Psychology." Esoteric Psychology shows you how to integrate your soul, your body, your personality, your mind and your spirit. Thus, you can advance quickly on your spiritual journey.

It is important to identify your specific rays, particularly your soul ray, so that you can implement your special talents and gifts in your best means of expression, rather than trying to emulate a path that is not yours and diluting your self-expression. Knowing your specific rays and using the tools provided in this book will empower you with dynamic focus, discrimination, and balance. The study of the Twelve Rays enables us to focus on the strengths of our particular ray(s) and be aware of the pitfalls and challenges. It gives us greater insight into our divine mission and central purpose for this incarnation. We can then understand the true meaning of our lives.

Chapter 4

How the Rays Influence Us

Each individual is comprised of several different rays. Each one of us has the following:

- **Physical Body Ray Number**
- **Emotional Body Ray Number**
- **Mental Body Ray Number**
- **Personality Ray Number**
- **Soul Ray Number**
- **Monad Ray Number**

Throughout this book, I will be presenting information on the various rays to assist you in determining what your individual ray numbers are on all of these levels.

As you proceed through this book, you may choose to fill in the following information for yourselves as you determine your ray numbers:

My Physical Body Ray Number_____

My Emotional Body Ray Number_____

My Mental Body Ray Number_____

My Personality Ray Number_____

My Soul Ray Number_____

My Monad Ray Number_____

These rays powerfully affect every human being's life. The *physical body ray* greatly determines the physical features of the body. The *emotional body ray* affects the quality of the emotions, and the *mental body ray* greatly determines the nature of the mind. The *personality ray* finds its major activity in the physical body and causes the attitude of separateness. The *soul ray* specifically influences the astral (emotional) body and facilitates the attitude of group consciousness—as well as detachment from the form side of life. The *monadic ray* (which can only be felt after the third initiation) is especially influential in the mental body and brings in the will aspect of the Creator.

We develop our awareness of these rays in the following order: physical, emotional, mental, personality, soul and monad rays. Because these rays predispose us to certain strengths and weaknesses, knowledge of our particular rays is absolutely essential in order to know ourselves. For example, certain characteristics of mind are easy for one ray type and very difficult for another. This is why we change our ray structure from life to life until we have mastered *all* of the ray qualities (virtues, aspects, and attributes of the Creator) and brought them into our essence.

The rays of the physical, emotional and mental bodies dominate at first in each person's life. As the person evolves and develops a more self-actualized personality, then the personality ray becomes dominant; the three-body rays (physical, emotional and mental) then become subordinate to the personality.

After further evolvement, the person becomes polarized in the soul. There is usually a battle or conflict, which occurs between the lower self (the personality ray) and the higher self (the soul ray). The personality ray becomes subordinate to the soul ray as the person begins to gain self-mastery.

The monadic ray begins to pour in after the third initiation. This begins the process of the soul ray becoming subordinate to the monadic ray.

We can utilize all of the rays whether we have them in our ray structure or not. We can call forth any of the twelve rays and their qualities for personal and planetary service. There are some rules in doing so, however: 1) It is *not* appropriate to send any ray to an individual or individuals without their permission or request. 2) It is permissible to send rays for planetary service provided that you *never send Ray One or Ray Four energy to the planet.* This is because Ray One is too explosive and powerful; it has the potential of great destruction. Ray Four is too volatile emotionally and could cause tremendous imbalance, chaos and havoc.

We can use various rays to balance ourselves. For example, if we are feeling too emotional, we can call in Ray Five to bring in more of a mental focus. A very tiny amount of Ray One energy is helpful when we are traumatized by our emotions. Wearing red can help us attune to this energy. (This is a powerful ray and must be used with caution in the appropriate amount.) First Ray people who are harsh and cruel need to be tempered with the Second Ray of love and wisdom. Fourth Ray types who have gotten too entangled with the emotional body benefit by calling in and working with the first, third and fifth ray, which are more mental in nature and provide balance. In addition, if we are needing certain attributes for balance or specific projects, we can call in the appropriate rays for those qualities: We can call in Ray One for more power, Ray Two for more love and wisdom, Ray Three for more action, Ray Four for more artistic inspiration and creativity, Ray Five for a scientific or mathematical approach, Ray Six for more devotion and Ray Seven for an emphasis on business. We can invoke any of the twelve rays through intention and the use of their respective colors.

Chapter 5

The following table illustrates the relationship of the Twelve Rays.

The Twelve Rays

Rays of Aspect	Rays of Attribute	Higher Rays
1st Ray of Power/Will/Purpose	4th Ray of Harmony through Conflict/Beauty and Art	8th Ray of Cleansing Blend of Rays 4, 5, 7 + Light
2nd Ray of Love/Wisdom	5th Ray of Concrete Science or Knowledge	9th Ray of Joy & loosens ties to physical plane Blend of Rays 1 & 2 + Light
3rd Ray of Active, Creative Intelligence	6th Ray of Abstract Idealism or Devotion	10th Ray codes the body of Light into the physical structure Blend of Rays 1, 2, & 3 + Light
	7th Ray of Ceremonial Order, Magic, Ritual, or Organization	11th Ray—Bridge to the New Age Blend of Rays 1, 2, & 5 + Light
		12th Ray-embodies all the Rays but not in equal proportions — anchors the Light consciousness on Earth.

Notes

Chapter 6

The Seven Physical Bodies

The ray of the physical body is the easiest to determine because its characteristics can be seen early in life. As you read through the following descriptions of the seven different types of physical bodies, keep in mind that you may have characteristics from more than one group and you will probably not have all of the characteristics in any one group. This is normal; one ray is dominant, however.

Ray One: The Ray One Physical Body is full of nervous energy in its electro-magnetic field. People with Ray One physical bodies get anxious quickly and are very wiry. They do not like any kind of fans or wind on them as it makes them sick. They do not particularly like to eat, need lots of protein and tend to have problems with anemia at various times in their lives. They push themselves and are constantly in motion. Ray One physical bodies are active and also possess a sense of isolation. Wherever they are, they need their own space. Ray One people move quickly, walk straight, do not lean, and walk on the balls of their feet. They are very alert and mentally active. They tend to be fairly tall for their family size, strongly built, have deeply-set eyes, possess wrists and hands that are large for their bodies, do not slump over, and have very slim shoulders and hips. Despite the fact that they do not sleep much, they get healthier and younger looking as they get older. They are happy with their bodies, and you cannot make them sit still. A first-ray body wills its way through anything.

Ray Two: Ray Two physical bodies are rather unusual and rare, although more will be incarnating in the future. They can be described as Little Bo Peep. They are very small with tender skin and exquisite features. Their skin is translucent, and they have tiny feet and hands. They can get heavy very quickly; but, if they gain weight, their feet and hands stay the same size. They are good at dancing and are not athletic. They like to sit and be waited on. Ray Two bodies have a certain amount of fat and cannot take very much food. They love beautiful jewelry and soft materials. They tend to have dimples in interesting spots. They go through puberty early, are prone to asthma and allergies, and have a low pain threshold. Their blood vessels are extremely small. They are physically frail, but strong emotionally. They should not get chilled.

People with Ray Two physical bodies should realize that they cannot handle as much physical stress as the other rays can, and they need to be protective of their delicate constitution. They are very refined and sensitive with the gift of awareness.

People with Ray Two physical bodies can sometimes change their bodies to Ray Three or Ray Seven by going on an exercise program and eating more carbohydrates. They need sodium and more mineral intake to change to a Ray Seven body.

Ray Three: The Ray Three body represents an athletic individual who likes to wear easy, comfortable clothing. Three-fourths of Americans are of the Ray Three body. Ray Threes must have lots of carbohydrates, such as potatoes, pasta, etc. They are either very active or they "flop." They grow at a steady rate. Alcohol is a major problem. Sports are important. They are not exceptionally tall and are medium-size in proportion. Ray Threes are energetic when they want to be. They like people and affection and the family unit. The Ray Three body can go through lots of changes. If they are over-energized and overdo things, they can damage their hearts. Ray Threes are basically healthy and happy. They can put on weight, and chocolate is very important to them. Their bodies do not contain much sodium or potassium unless these substances are added.

Ray Four: There are currently no Ray Four Bodies on earth as they have been gone since the 16th century. These people were the "blue-skinned" ones with blue eyes, translucent skin and dark hair. They were very daring and very charismatic people who liked doing things for the sake of doing them. They had longer faces. They were very flirtatious, dressed up, and were written about in legend. Ray Four Bodies will be coming back in 2025.

Ray Five: Ray Five bodies are very rare. They are equally proportioned between their heads, torsos and legs. They are mostly found in the mountains of China and Tibet. They have a tendency to walk rabbit-like with jerky movements. They have short arms and legs, and their heads look large. They have very little hair growth over their body. Dwarfs fall into this category, but this category is not limited to dwarfs. Ray Five bodies must be careful of their vitamin levels. They tend to lose more calcium. The Ray Five body is best for space ships.

Ray Six: Ray Six bodies are soft. They hold fluids and love to be touched. They cannot take heat or earth changes. They cannot take discomfort and find life to be stressful. People with Ray Six physical bodies perspire copiously and have larger amounts of fluid and lithium in their bodies. They love to "mother" people. The Ray Six physical bodies show happy people with many compulsive behavior patterns. They can enjoy being sick. They have small hands and feet and go through puberty early. They like to wear fun and interesting clothes and tend to have larger or heavier bodies. They like fabrics and materials that are soft. They like to touch and be touched, and are very social. They make good healers and beauticians.

Ray Seven: Ray Seven bodies often display shoulders and hips that are the same size, giving them the tendency to have a "straight-up-and-down" look. They are from the Greek incarnation. They mature late, if ever. Ray Seven bodies can take sun and heat. They have long legs, grow rapidly, and generally stay thin. They have trouble with their joints. Some of the seven-foot basketball players are of the Ray Seven body. Ray

Sevens have balanced mineral salts and get healthier as they get older. They are able to withstand the earth changes. They do not like to be touched very much and are very health-conscious. Many of them do not like sports and exercise. They are very attuned to order and love uniforms. They are incarnating in droves. Ray Sevens often have an androgynous look.

Notes

Chapter 7

The Seven Emotional Bodies

The goal in Esoteric (Spiritual) Psychology is to merge the personality with the soul. In order to do this, the elimination of glamour and illusion is necessary. In the Second Initiation, disciples go through many experiences to purify their emotions and become clear for the light of the soul to shine through unobstructed. It takes many lifetimes (possibly hundreds of incarnations) to change an emotional body type to a different ray or purify the glamour and illusions of that level.

The following is a brief description of some of the emotional characteristics of the various rays. The emotional body ray becomes apparent in childhood and is fairly easy to identify.

Ray One: Divine Will and Power. To the Ray One person, self-rule or self-dependence is happiness. Rule by others is misery. Ray One people look at the world as a land of adventure for the valiant will, the sunny heart or the aspiring mind. They are full of initiative and do not look upon the world as a teacher, but as a place to create and perform deeds of prowess. They deliberately use their intuition and own faculties of thought and feeling in the game of life, and they grow by that exercise. Their sense of self is strong; they have a firmness amid things and events that scarcely anything in the world can shake or change, an inclination to be positive in action, and the courage to face life as an adventure and not take refuge or rest amid things. They have power and flexibility, dignity of the self and live for the expression of their inner self, which is the center and balancing point of their being.[5]

Ray One people may appear to be aloof and struggle with pride. They judge their status—either in the masses or on the spiritual ladder. They are clear, objective, aloof, honest, humble, and accepting of where they are in life. They are not cold, as they have consideration and can be trusted.

Some of the "vices" or misapplied First Ray energy could include pride, ambition, willfulness, hardness, arrogance, desire to control others, obstinacy, and anger.

Special virtues of the Ray One Emotional body are strength, courage, steadfastness, truthfulness arising from absolute fearlessness, power of ruling capacity to grasp great questions in a large-minded way, and handling people and situations. The highest manifestation is true humility. Virtues to be acquired are tenderness, humility, sympathy, tolerance, and patience.

Ray Two: Love/Wisdom. Ray Two Emotional Bodies are rare and can be described as peaceful, stable and mature. They are truly compassionate and impersonal. They love everyone and everything—just as the sun shines on everything, not just what it selects as "worthy" of its light. They take the whole universe into consideration. They share and rarely (if ever) have jealousy, despair, or ups-and-downs. They have no personal anger, but they can have universal anger.

The characteristic of the second ray is love, the positive expression in life of that wisdom which perceives through sympathy the state of consciousness in other beings, and takes it into account in dealing with them. It is also a ray of initiative because love is the active energy of the soul, and all its activities tend to promote brotherhood and make our unity with one another more complete in this life.

Ray Two people are as interested in the lives of others as much as their own. Their love flows out of altruism; they are willing to suffer for their love and are ready to face the world with all of its imperfections and its mixture of pleasures and pains, and humbly say, "Only

God is good, and all this is just better or worse." They have room for rejoicing at all times because the "worse" is always becoming better and because every act of kindness, of comradeship or service serves the betterment of all, which will at last lead to that which is "good." They believe in the doctrine of the evolution of life as upward and onward forever. Their beliefs flow into neighborliness and brotherhood.

They must at times be careful to not give too much help to others at the expense of their own resources or preventing the people they are helping from growing and developing on their own. An example of this would be that it is all right to lift a lame dog over a stile, but it may be foolish and unkind to carry it all along the road.[6]

Distorted emotional energy on Ray Two could show over-absorption in study, coldness, indifference to others, and contempt of the mental limitations of others.

Special virtues of Ray Two are calmness, strength, patience, endurance, love of truth, faithfulness, intuition, clear intelligence, a serene temperament, love, compassion, unselfishness and energy. The highest manifestation is compassion.

Ray Three: Active Intelligence. The Ray Three Emotional Bodies are objective and lacking in ambition. They are sensitive to things in the interests of consciousness. They are philosophers who want understanding or comprehension and feel that happiness depends upon that; even if the world might pour its bounty lavishly upon men and all are at peace in brotherhood, happiness would be lacking if there were no means of understanding the significance of all these things to the soul.

Ray Three people are cautious. They want information on which their thoughts may be soundly based. They can think so carefully about things that they lose the opportunity before they decide what to do.

The power of this ray gives people a very broad mind, freedom from compulsion, and a wide range of opportunity. Sometimes people with this ray have difficulty sorting out and narrowing down what they need to focus on in their lives. This can prevent them from becoming what some might call "successful" in life.

In facing the problems of life, Ray Three people will say, "The truth will make us free. Give us understanding—action is bound to follow, so we need not worry about it. Whether the truth is painful or pleasant, we want it. Never mind our feelings." If they fail in love or in action, they do not feel ruined: but a failure in truth will give them bitter remorse. Ray Three people have adaptability.

Distorted Ray Three energy could manifest as intellectual pride, coldness, isolation, inaccuracy in details, absent-mindedness, obstinacy, selfishness, and much criticism of others.

Special virtues of Ray Three include wide views on all abstract questions, sincerity of purpose, clear intellect, capacity for concentration on philosophic studies, patience, caution, absence of the tendency to worry themselves or others over trifles, sympathy, tolerance, devotion, accuracy, energy, and common sense. The highest manifestation of Ray Three is Good Will.

Ray Four: Harmony Through Conflict. Ray Four Emotional Bodies stir things up. It excites their adrenal glands to stir everybody up, and they are hard to live with. They have insatiable curiosity, and they can goad people on just to see what their reactions will be. They feed on arguing. The positive side of this is that they bring people out of their apathy, motivating them to be creative and to think. Sometimes, however, they can be deliberately malicious.

Distorted Ray Four energy shows up in the following characteristics: self-centeredness, worrying, inaccuracy, lack of moral courage, strong passions, indolence (idleness and laziness) and extravagance. When Fourth Ray people get into conflict, they become very compulsive, self-feeding, creating a roller-coaster effect of going from the heights and then to the depths.

Ray Four special virtues include strong affections, sympathy, physical courage, generosity, devotion, quickness of intellect, perception, serenity, confidence, self-control, purity, unselfishness, accuracy, mental and moral balance. The highest manifestations of Ray Four are beauty and harmony, moderation and poise.

Ray Five: Concrete Knowledge or Science. Ray Five emotional bodies are very rare and too scientific. They represent concrete science and are totally impersonal. They can be harsh, cut-and-dried, dealing only with pure mathematical concepts and the collection of facts.

Distortion of Ray Five energy results in harsh criticism, narrowness, arrogance, unforgiving temper, lack of sympathy and reverence, and prejudice.

Special virtues of Ray Five include strictly accurate statements, justice (without mercy), perseverance, common sense, uprightness, independence, keen intellect, reverence, devotion, sympathy, love, and wide-mindedness. The highest manifestation of Ray Five is pure honesty.

Ray Six: Abstract Idealism or Devotion. Ray Six Emotional Bodies get excited about people. They build backgrounds to support the effect. This is a very "Hollywood, glamour and illusion" ray. Ray Six people are compulsive. They depend upon others to be satiated and satisfied. They can be very warm, like to share, like to hug, and enjoy people on a one-to-one basis. Ray Six people want to be "high." They must have somebody else to be complete. They cannot be complete by themselves.

Touching, holding hands, expressing affection is very important to them. They experience sexual satisfaction and dissatisfaction at the same time. For example, they may say, "I felt loved, and when it was all over, I didn't feel loved." They often experience jealousy. They are very excitable and often overly active in their beliefs. Distorted Ray Six energy can result in the following: selfish and jealous love, leaning too much on others, partiality, self-deception, sectarianism, superstition, prejudice, over-rapid conclusions, and fiery anger.

Ray Six special virtues include devotion, single-mindedness, love, tenderness, intuition, loyalty, reverence, strength, self-sacrifice, purity, truth, tolerance, serenity, balance and common sense. The highest manifestation of Ray Six is impersonality.

Ray Seven: Ceremonial Order or Magic. Ray Seven represents ceremonial order and magic. Ray Seven people like to build through the power of thought and take personal delight in "all things done decently and in order" and according to rule and precedent. It is the ray of the high priest, the genius in organizations, the perfect nurse for the sick, careful in the smallest detail, although sometimes too much inclined to disregard the patient's idiosyncrasies. It is the ray of the perfect sculptor and designer of beautiful forms.[7]

Ray Seven people are fluent in writing and speech. As writers they are more concerned about the polished style than the material they are writing about. Ray Sevens delight in great processions and shows, genealogical trees and rules of precedence. They are determined to do the right thing at the right moment, which makes for great social success.

On the other hand, superstitions and deep interest in omens, dreams, and spiritualistic phenomena are serious drawbacks. Because magic can stimulate their lower nature, there is danger of swinging into a maelstrom of work, in which they are materially-minded, selfishly ambitious and unloving.

Ray Seven shows the love of order, ritual and sometimes confusion as to where they should focus their attention.

Distorted Ray Seven energy can result in formalism, bigotry, pride, narrowness, superficial judgments, overindulgence in self-opinions, fragmentation, and the desire to manipulate others.

Special virtues of Ray Seven are strength, perseverance, courage, extreme care in details, self-reliance, courtesy, realization of unity, wide-mindedness, tolerance, humility, gentleness and love. The highest manifestation of Ray Seven is a sense of purpose.

Notes

Chapter 8

The Seven Mental Bodies

The **Mental Body** is the vehicle through which you contact the universal wisdom. Whereas we can sometimes change the physical body ray number in one life, it takes hundreds of years to change the emotional body ray number and thousands of years to change the mental body ray number. The Mental Body Ray Number is what ties us to Ashramic Groups (of which there are seven) and clusters of people. It is very spiritual. The Fourth, Fifth, and Seventh Ray Mental Bodies are increasing. Keep in mind that we *modify* our behavior in order to live in society, so you may find characteristics that you resonate to in more than one ray number. One number is predominant, however. To determine the ray of your mental body, check the following clues.

The Mental Body Ray can usually be identified by the time of adolescence.

Ray One: Ray One Mental Bodies see truth in concrete matter. Facts speak to them, and they are concerned with organization and cataloging. They administrate, put things in order, and work towards a goal in an established order. They are methodical, and they use their minds to suppress emotion. They are interested in cycles, functions within a masculine hierarchy or complex. This would be represented by the trinity rather than a circle. Ray One Mental Bodies appreciate the chain of command and let the student stand alone. They look for steps, patterns, and logic in the repetition of cycles. They tend to be militaristic and are often found in the areas of government and history. Kings, queens and wars appeal to them. They do not tend to argue or go into great discussions. Ray Ones are more interested in statistics than descriptions. They do not look at alternate realities until they are proven. Gandhi and Napoleon are represented in the Ray One Mental Body.

Ray Two: Ray Two Mental Bodies are very receptive, and they are concerned with civilizations, peoples, and group situations. Major concerns of theirs are how do you change the thinking of a nation and how and why do cultures evolve? These issues are not viewed from a personal standpoint, only as how cycles interweave. They share all knowledge and wisdom and inspire and wonder about life. Their teaching methods often include asking thoughtful questions, and they flow with the crowd itself. They often use parables and stories to teach, according to what the students and groups can understand. They are concerned with the cause and effect of change. Their ideas are broad, not factual and personal. Robert Louis Stevenson is an example of a Ray Two Mental Body.

Ray Three: Ray Three Mental Bodies are contemplative and philosophical. They look behind the slogans and the claims, and make adjustments. They tend to be brooding and deep into thought. They often float through their subject matter and become what they study. Ray Threes look at the past to understand the future. They are not necessarily "going anywhere" with what they study; they just want to understand it. They are often accused of not being mentally alert. Their perspective says, "Now is all there is. I observe now." They are philosophers, and only a small percentage of the population (under 10 percent) fall into this category. Henry David Thoreau and some Native Americans are examples of Ray Three mental bodies.

Ray Four: Most people are Ray Four Mental Bodies. They are creative and artistic. They teach through dramatization, personal examples, illustration, and the use of visual aids. Ray Fours are concerned with personal consciousness. They want you to get the importance of any principle and frequently give you hints in order to achieve this. They see language as an art form and love to play with words. Ray Fours play upon people's moods and feelings and are constantly adjusting for this. They have good teaching patterns. Over half the world's population are Ray Four Mental Bodies, and there are more in the Western Hemisphere.

Ray Five: Ray Five Mental Bodies are best associated with the Scientific Method. They analyze everything and are predominantly mathematical in their orientation. They use initials, symbols, cause and effect, and verified facts as their foundations. Ray Fives think in numbers. True Astrology (without the mythology) and computers fall under the Ray Five Mental Body. Ray Fives are interested in pure logic and need to prove things. They are not personal; in their thinking, experiments have to be repeated because nothing is sure. Their written expression usually manifests as a table with numbers. They express and respond visually and on paper to life. They are not auditory. Ray Fives tend to cluster together and separate themselves from those who do not understand them. They are very close with each other, but they separate themselves from the rest of the world. Albert Einstein and other real scientists are examples of the Ray Five Mental Body.

The world is basically divided between the Ray Four and the Ray Five mind, with the Ray Four seeing life with language and the Ray Five seeing life with numbers.

Ray Six: There are currently no Ray Six Mental Bodies.

Ray Seven: Ray Seven Mental Bodies see life as a big joke. They "play people like a game." They use subliminal tactics, invoking and evoking powers. They repeat patterns and are future-oriented. They deal with the subconscious mind and control people's minds. They build illusions and evade the world and the system. They are *different*—not necessarily good or bad. They are normal and not malicious and see mind control as normal. There are not many Ray Seven Mental Bodies. The joker in the movie *Batman*, played by Jack Nicholson, would be an example of a Ray Seven Mental Body.

Notes

Chapter 9

The Seven Personality Rays

It is important to differentiate between the personality and the soul. The *personality* is the composite of the cloak for incarnation—the way in which we relate to other people and our outer shell. We can change the personality ray within one lifetime. The personality ray can be compared to clothing for the body or a mask; it is our personal identity for one life. The *soul ray* almost never changes. It is the divine expression of the soul.

It is also important to distinguish between the mental body, which is the highest aspect of the personality, and the soul. The *mental body* deals with knowledge, particulars, or what are called concrete thoughts—for instance, a particular tree, car or triangle. The mental body is the instrument for concrete thinking and expresses concrete thoughts through the physical brain. In contrast, the *soul* is concerned with principles or abstract thoughts: trees or cars in general or the principle of triangularity common to all triangles. The soul is the instrument for abstract thinking and is the storehouse for the abstracted essence, or wisdom, gained from experiences. Due to the presence of the soul, a human being is able to have *self-consciousness* and develop *group consciousness*.[8]

Following birth, a human being learns to integrate the etheric body with the physical body, the emotional body with the etheric body, and then the mental body with the emotional body. After learning how to coordinate all aspects of the personality, we begin the process of integrating the personality with the soul. This last stage of integration takes the individual through certain expansions of awareness that are called initiations. We can relate each initiation to increased activity in a specific chakra.

The process of integrating personality with the soul is intuitively guided by the soul. Because there are seven basic types of souls, there are seven basic processes of integration—one for each ray.

The following is a brief description of the characteristics of the personality rays.

Ray One Personality: Ray One personalities have dignity and a strong sense of self. They have a personal plan for their lives, and they are prepared to carry it out. They are courageous people who take action and linear steps to achieve their goals. Ray One personalities are at all times aware of which rung of the ladder they are on in their climb to the top. They take one step at a time and will find a way around any obstacles that get in the way of achieving their goal(s).

Ray One is the Ray of Will and Power. The basic quality for persons on this ray is dynamic purpose and the basic technique is grasping what they need. Their will power is strong, for either good or evil. This power works out as strength, courage and steadfastness. It embodies the *creator/destroyer principle:* We must tear down the existing structures and forms to build new ones.

Ray one personalities are born leaders, generally found at the head of their professions. Many outstanding sports figures are of this type. As soldiers, Ray One personalities would be commanders-in-chief. They rarely are artists. Possible careers could include government, politics, international relations, executive activities, statesmanship, diplomacy, military, exploration, etc., but Ray One personalities are not limited to the above career choices.

The descriptive animal for the Ray One personality is the camel.

Ray Two Personality: Ray Two personalities are conscious of the people they are with. They are calm and compassionate. These people can enjoy things without possessing them. Life is circular to them. They do not have excessive need of anything; therefore, they tend to not be jealous or philosophical or ambitious.

The Second Ray is called the Ray of Love/Wisdom. Second Ray personalities can experience the following: They intuitively sense the basic quality of the soul, which is inclusive love, and then contrast this quality with the anger, hatred, and bitterness of their interpersonal relationships. Since the old way of relating with people resulted in disappointment, they wonder whether there is a better way and how they might find that way. They begin to seek answers by closely studying from various books, teachers and teachings, which provide an outer confirmation of their own evolving understanding.

Ray Two personalities see themselves as a point within a circle as well as an individual at the same time. Ultimately, in their highest expression, the love of love must dominate, not the love of being loved.

The Second Ray carries with it the law of magnetic impulse. Probable careers and vocations for Ray Two personalities could include, but are certainly not limited to, the following: education, healing, writing, speaking, television, intuitive speaking, and the study of religion.

The animal that is representative of the Ray Two personality is the cow.

Ray Three Personality: Ray Three personalities see how things *should be.* They believe that the truth shall make us free. They do not necessarily *do* things; sometimes they just *think* about them. They are theorists and idealistic dreamers. The non-enlightened Ray Three personalities are couch potatoes; they are observers in life. Ray Three personalities do not usually take a stand. They are abstract and often perfectionists. They exist and they observe. The majority of Ray Three personalities are located in the Eastern Hemisphere. Many live in Tibet.

Ray Three represents Active Intelligence and the Law of Expansive Response. To Ray Three personalities, the love of truth must dominate, not the love of their own thoughts or the love of their own ideas or forms. Love of the ordered process must control, not the love of their own wild activity. They learn to stand silent, quiet and unafraid and not rush from point to point. They are not deluded by the outer forms and that which disappears. They search for the weaver within. This is a ray of adaptability and perseverance.

Possible careers for Ray Three personalities could include, but are not limited to, the following: finance, trade, business, economics, travel, communication, philosophy, astrology, and all scholarly pursuits.

The elephant is the animal that is representative of Ray Three personalities.

Ray Four Personality: To the Ray Four personality, all ideas must be given expression. These personalities say that you can pretend to be anything that you want. They are very artistic on a personal level. Ray Fours can be prone to escapism if they do not like what is happening. They must verbalize, and they want to tell you their ideas and ideals. They enjoy playing games, gossiping, and being creative. They are mostly talk with little action. (Interestingly, our government does this, and as a nation we are predominantly Ray Four.)

Because Ray Four people enjoy such a powerful connection to the Earth, they frequently find it difficult to meditate or focus on the spiritual side of life. Ray Fours are usually very physically active, participating in Earth living and activities such as hiking, mountain climbing, horseback riding, driving of vehicles and relating to animals. This is fine as long as it is balanced with heavenly and spiritual integration. If they do not develop their spiritual approach to life, there is a danger of them being manipulative and tending towards manic-depression.

Ray Four personalities stand between the forces, which oppose each other and long for harmony and peace and the beauty that results from unity.

Ray Four represents the Law of Harmony through Conflict and the Law of Sacrifice. The basic quality of a Fourth-Ray individual is harmony and synthesis, and the basic technique is unifying the forces in the environment. This ray is also called the "ray of struggle' because individuals on this ray often have personalities that are torn between conflicting tendencies, such as the love of ease, pleasure, indolence, and procrastination on the one hand and fiery impatience and urge to action on the other. They may be wild speculators and gamblers who are full of enthusiasm and plans, become easily overwhelmed by failure, but quickly recover from their misfortunes. As soldiers, they would tend to disregard risks to themselves and their followers; as artists, their sense of color would be great, but their drawing might be defective; as musicians, their music would be full of melody; and as writers, their literary work would often be brilliant and full of picturesque word-paintings but might be inaccurate and full of exaggerations.[9]

When this ray is governed by the lower self, then conflict and havoc ensue. When it is governed by the higher self, harmony occurs.

Careers for Ray Four personalities might include, but are certainly not limited to, the following: sociology, cooperative endeavors, art, conciliation, creative aspiration, refining, manipulation (beauty is an expression of truth.)

The monkey is the animal of the Ray Four personality.

Ray Five Personality: Ray Five personalities live by the laws of nature and obey them. They are very close to animals—more so than people—and see truth in nature. They are helping the animal kingdom for the next step.

The Fifth Ray represents Concrete Knowledge or Science. Individuals on this ray have a thirst for knowledge and are by nature scientific researchers. Either as vocation or avocation, they find problems to study. Their efforts are aimed at comprehending the meanings and relationships that lie beyond their present understanding. Thus, they are working toward what could be characterized as expansion, inclusion, and enlightenment. This ray likes schedules and usually won't change. They are fascinated with form.

Possible careers for Ray Five personalities could include, but are not limited to the following: planning, designing, science, psychology, modern education, mathematics, and areas of concentration, such as Yoga.

The animal representative of Ray Five is the horse.

Ray Six Personality: Ray Six personalities are zealous about what they do. **The Sixth Ray is called the Ray of Devotion and Idealism.**

Ray Six personalities make excellent soldiers and do well in the military because they follow orders very well. Their philosophy is "I need to follow." Ray Six personalities are patriotic, believe in good and bad, spiritual versus evil, are religious, and tend to see life in "black and white " with little "gray." These people believe that there are many vices and virtues and tend to put labels on everything.

A charming phenomenon is that many people who like dogs and dress them up with bows in their hair, etc., are Ray Six personalities.

Possible careers for Ray Six could include, but are not limited to the following: religion, ideology, the military, philosophy, preaching, church work, oration, and evangelism.

The animal that is representative of Ray Six is the dog.

Ray Seven Personality: Ray Seven personalities work within certain laws, but are not like Ray Fives. Ray Sevens say that man and nature can both be manipulated. Houdini is a good example of a Ray Seven personality.

Ray Sevens focus on the etheric (see Glossary at end of book) body rather than the physical body. Metals, minerals and candles are important to them. They believe that the end justifies the means. They believe that they are standing in the field of magic and are here to create forms and carry out the divine plans of creation. They are workers in the fields of magic.

Ray Seven represents Ceremonial Order or Magic and the Law of Transmutation. Ray Seven personalities are often found in the following fields (but not limited to these): white magic, spiritualism, priesthood, parades, protocol, parliamentary procedures, ritual, and ceremony.

The animal that is representative of Ray Seven is the cat.

Notes

Chapter 10

The Seven Soul Rays

The Soul Ray almost never changes. The following is a brief description of the rays as they pertain to the soul. It is important to emphasize that the actual qualities that we display depend on our point of evolution. Because the qualities listed at the end of each ray are characteristic of the **soul, we can display them only if we are starting to become integrated with the soul and live as the soul.** But, if we are still focused in the personality and living in the personality, then our characteristics could reflect the direct opposite of the qualities listed. The following characteristics describe souls who are able to experience the level of group consciousness and have moved beyond just the individual personality.

Ray One Soul: **Ray One is the Ray of Will and Power.** It embodies the creator/destroyer concept and can be described as singular, masculine, and attuned to the past. The basic quality for persons on this ray is dynamic purpose, and the basic technique is grasping what they need. Their will power is strong—for either good or evil. This power works out as strength, courage and steadfastness, but it also can work out as a destructive force with an apparent cruelty and impersonality. This is the **creator/destroyer principle:** We must tear down outmoded existing structures and forms to build new ones.

First-ray persons often have strong feelings and affections, but do not readily express them. They are born leaders, generally found at the head of their professions. As soldiers, they would be able commanders-in-chief. They rarely are artists. As writers, their literary works would be strong and trenchant with little regard for style and polish.[10]

There is no true Ray One **soul** in incarnation as yet. Ray One will come into full play when the time comes for the divine purpose to be safely revealed. All so-called Ray One souls are on the **first sub-ray of the second Cosmic Ray**, which is in incarnation.

Viewed symbolically, Ray One embodies the dynamic idea of God, and thus the Most High starts the work of creation.

Qualities of Ray One: singleness of purpose, dynamic power, clear vision, detachment, solitariness, sense of time.

Ray Two Soul: **Ray Two is the ray of Love and Wisdom.** This ray is represented by compassion, non-personal love, and healing. Ray Two souls see life as a circle and anyone who wants to join is welcomed. There is a sense of timelessness that does not focus on ambition and drive.

The basic quality for individuals on this ray is inclusive love, and the basic technique is attracting what one needs. They have a desire for knowledge and truth, are more magnetic than dynamic, and are builders rather than destroyers. They generally have tact, foresight and the ability to convey understanding to others. They may be excellent ambassadors, psychotherapists, teachers or college heads. As soldiers, they would plan wisely and never lead their troops into danger through rashness; but they may be deficient in rapidity of action and energy. Artists on this ray would seek to teach through their art. As writers, their literary work would generally be instructive.[11]

Qualities of Ray Two: Love Divine, attraction, radiance, power to save, expansion or inclusiveness, wisdom.

Ray Three Soul: **Ray Three is the Ray of Active Intelligence and Adaptability.** It represents the Divine Mother, the Goddess, and the objective feminine. It is non-personal and is the ray of the observer. Ray Three souls observe history and believe in the concept of the "right thing at the right moment." They almost become non-entities with their detachment, believing that nothing really **exists**. This is the ray of the diplomat, the archetype of the old Japanese and Chinese philosophers.

The basic quality of a person on the third ray is intellect, and the basic technique is selectively manipulating the elements of the environment. Persons on this ray have a highly developed imagination and can grasp the essence of a truth by the power of this faculty. Due to their wide views and great caution, they often see every side of a question equally clearly, which sometimes paralyzes their actions. They may be good abstract thinkers, philosophers and business people. As soldiers, they would work out tactical problems at their desks, but would seldom be outstanding on the field. As artists, their subjects would be full of thought and interest, but their techniques may not be polished. As writers, their literary style would often be vague and involved.[12]

Qualities of Ray Three: mental illumination, power to manifest, scientific investigation, power to evolve, balance, and power to produce synthesis on the physical plane.

Ray Four Soul: **Ray Four is the Ray of Harmony through Conflict and Beauty and Art.** The basic quality of a fourth-ray individual is harmony and synthesis, and the basic technique is unifying the forces in the environment. This ray is also called the "ray of struggle" because individuals on this ray often have personalities that are torn between conflicting tendencies, such as the love of pleasure, ease, indolence, and procrastination on the one hand and fiery impatience and urge to action on the other.

The souls of this ray are artists and creative people who constantly search for perfection. There is an ever-present tension in this ray as the search for perfection (true harmony) is what makes us criticize. Beethoven, Chopin and Baryshnikov are examples of Ray Four souls. Ray Four souls are perfectionists. They do not go to groups; instead they have personal trainers. They want the whole world to be perfect, and they live in torment because this is not possible. The Olympic ice skaters and some performing artists fall into this ray. There are many Ray Four souls in Russia. Many Ray Four souls are coming back into incarnation. Some of the souls on this ray kill themselves because it is too frustrating and difficult for them to be in incarnation.

As mentioned earlier, Ray Four soldiers would tend to disregard risks to themselves and their followers. As artists, their sense of color would be great, but their drawing might be defective. As musicians, their music would be full of melody. As writers, their literary work would often be brilliant and full of picturesque word-paintings but might be inaccurate and full of exaggerations.

Qualities of Ray Four: power to penetrate the depths of matter, harmony of the spheres, synthesis of true beauty, dual aspects of desire, power to express divinity, power to reveal the path.

Ray Five Soul: **Ray Five is the Ray of Concrete Knowledge or Science.** It is totally impersonal, cut-and-dried, consisting of a collection of facts. Under this ray, there are no ambiguities and no misunderstandings. Everything is clear and structured, and everyone knows his or her role. Life is "black and white." Ray Five souls do not go to groups. They are the pure scientists, pure computer people, and the mathematicians. Mr. Spock from Star Trek is an example of a Ray Five soul.

The basic quality for individuals on this ray is discrimination, and the technique is differentiating the elements in their environment. As a result, they possess keen intellects, show accuracy in details, and make unwearied efforts to verify every theory. Other characteristics include being orderly, punctual, businesslike, and sometimes pedantic. They may be excellent scientists who analyze the material world in terms of causes and effects, or excellent electricians, engineers, or operating surgeons. As soldiers, they would be interested in artillery and engineering. As artists, which is extremely rare, their coloring would be dull, sculptures lifeless, and music uninteresting though technically correct in form. As writers, their style would show extreme clarity, lack of fire, and often long-windedness.[13]

Qualities of Ray Five: emergence into form and out of form, power to make the Voice of the Silence heard, manifestation of the great white light, revelation of the way, initiating activity, purification with fire.

Ray Six Soul: **Ray Six is the Ray of Devotion, Adoration and Idealism.** Souls under this ray want a "Guru" to worship. This is a soft and gentle ray, where souls are zealous and sympathetic. Ray Six souls are crusaders. They must have someone to follow or be the leader. There is absolute obedience under this ray.

The basic quality of individuals on this ray is sensitivity to the spiritual reality lying behind the phenomenal world. Their basic technique is devotional response, referring to a one-pointed application of desire and intelligence to produce an expression of the sensed idea. Consequently, the sixth ray is the ray of the devotee and the idealist. Individuals on this ray have intense personal feelings and religious instincts. They are seldom great statesmen or business people, but they may be great preachers or orators. As soldiers, they would hate fighting, but when aroused would fight with ferocity. As artists, they would be devoted to beauty and color, but their productivity skill may not be very good. As writers, they would be poets of the emotions, perhaps with a religious theme.[14]

Individuals on both the fourth and sixth rays are involved with the "pair of opposites," but with different kinds. The fourth-ray individual struggles with the pair of opposites in the form of dilemma: choosing between higher and lower ways of regarding some issue. The sixth-ray individual is involved with the pair of opposites in the form of partisanship.

Qualities of Ray Six: overcoming the waters of the emotional nature, endurance and fearlessness, power to kill out desire, self-immolation, spurning that which is not desired, power to detach oneself.

Ray Seven Soul: **Ray Seven is the ray of ceremonial magic and order.** These are the magical priests who manipulate the energies and are attuned to the future, not the past. Souls who manipulate minds and play with power fall into this ray. Many of these souls come from ancient Egypt.

The basic quality for individuals on the seventh ray is magic, which in this context means the ability to unify a mental image with the tangible form or appearance. Their basic technique is coordinating, blending and fusing the elements of the physical world. As a result, they take delight in doing things decently and in order, according to rule and precedent.

With their organizing power, seventh-ray individuals might be excellent business people. As soldiers, they would dress and feed the troops in the best possible way. As artists or sculptors, they would produce ideal beauty in material forms and patterns. As writers, their style would be ultra-polished, but they might be concerned more about style than content.[15]

Qualities of Ray Seven: power to create, power to think, mental power, power to vivify, power to cooperate, revelation of the beauty of God.

Notes

Chapter 11

The Monad Ray

The *Monad or Monadic Ray* is the primary ray that stays with each individual for eons. It does not change. This is the spiritual ray, the ray of our "I Am Presence." The "I AM Presence" can be defined as the higher self of your higher self, the part of you that merges with your soul at the time of ascension. It can also be described as your God Ray. The hierarchy of Ray levels is as follows:

> Monad
> Soul
> Personality
> Mental Plane
> Emotional Plane
> Physical Plane of Existence

The above diagram shows the *descending* order of importance, with the Monad level being the highest, and the physical plane being the lowest.

Everyone in existence has a Monad Ray of either one of the following:

> **Ray One: Divine Will and Power**
> **Ray Two: Love/Wisdom**
> **Ray Three: Active Intelligence**

Most people are not yet aware of their Monad Ray because they have not accessed and are not working at their Soul level or Monad level. When this evolvement takes place, they can determine their Monad Ray.

Notes

Chapter 12

Determining Your Soul Ray

The soul ray can be identified only after you have achieved some alignment with your soul and are utilizing some of your soul's powers. If such alignment and utilization are present, then you can do the following to aid in determining your soul ray:

1. **Consider your career.** Look at the approach taken to your career rather than your career itself. Which of the rays are reflected in your approach to your career? If you have shifted careers late in life, however, then that shift might indicate your soul ray. For example, if a person was formerly a creative artist but suddenly takes a deep and profound interest in mathematics, then it might be inferred that the influence of a second-ray or fifth-ray soul is becoming predominant.

2. **Examine your hobbies,** particularly those that you began after some alignment with your soul had been achieved. Generally speaking, our vocations indicate our personality ray, and our avocations indicate our soul ray. For example, if one pursues scientific investigation as a hobby, one might be responding to a fifth-ray soul.

3. **Look at the organizations** with which you are affiliated.

4. **Look at your personality,** your strengths and weaknesses, and the nature of your inner conflict.
5. **Let your intuition guide you** in determining your soul ray.

Note: It is easy to confuse the **personality ray** with the soul ray. Remember that the personality ray indicates your outer occupation or career, appearance, life-trend, goal and purpose. The **soul ray** indicates your basic quality and method of accomplishment.

Here is an example of what is meant by your **basic quality, approach and method of accomplishment:** Let us look at the career of a soldier. A first-ray personality may indicate the career of a soldier. An individual with any soul ray can be a soldier, but the approach to that career depends on the soul ray. For example, a first-ray soul would indicate leadership ability; a second-ray soul, wise planning during battle; a third-ray soul, an intellectual approach to military tactics; a fourth-ray soul, possible recklessness during combat; a fifth-ray soul, an interest in artillery and engineering; a sixth-ray soul, a ferocious fighter; and a seventh-ray soul, a good supply officer.[16]

Notes

Chapter 13

Rays Eight through Twelve

The Twelve Rays in all contain the attributes, aspects and virtues of our Father/Mother God or Creator.

Rays Eight through Twelve have a distinctly different purpose than Rays One through Seven. Rays Eight through Twelve present an opportunity to progress; thus, they enable man in the process of evolution back to the Source. Each of these higher galactic rays works in a unique and different way. Rays Eight through Twelve are blends of Rays One through Seven and are illuminated with the energy of wholeness and white crystalline Light of the Source.

Ray Eight

Ray Eight is the "Cleansing" Ray. It is a blend of Ray Four, Ray Five and Ray Seven. We can use Ray Eight to open the inner vision, bathe the emotional body and transmute the energy to a higher level. The color of this ray is a blend of luminous green and violet.

Ray Nine

Ray Nine is very useful in loosening the ties to the physical plane and establishing contact with the Soul level and Christed part of the

Self. This ray is a blend of Rays One and Two. The color is luminous light blue-green.

Joy is the main quality of the ninth ray.

Ray Ten

Ray Ten is a blend of the first, second, and third ray energies with the white Light of Wholeness added to it. Ray Ten codes the Body of Light into the physical body and helps us to lock in the changes that we wish to make. It helps facilitate the soul merge experience. The color is luminescent pearl.

Ray Eleven

Ray Eleven is the bridge to the next level for humanity and Earth itself. The color is a luminous orange-pink with the white Light of the Source added it. Ray Eleven is a blend of Rays One, Two, and Five. This ray removes the final remnants of what needs to be cleared to bring us to the next level.

Ray Twelve

Ray Twelve is a combination of all of the rays and all possibilities. The color is luminous gold. This is the focus of the highest type of energy that is available on Earth—the Mahatma energy from Source to Earth. Although Ray Twelve is a combination of all of the rays, there is a major concentration of the First Ray magnified by the Third Ray.

Ray Twelve is the ray of anchoring the Christ consciousness on Earth. This ray helps to promote inner realization, clears up confusion and enhances proper understanding and insight. Ray Twelve is the summit of all the higher rays.

Notes

Chapter 14

A Case Study

So far, we have just looked at the Seven Rays as a separate study. I would now like to show you their importance in the composite life of an individual person. How do the Seven Rays fit into our lives, and why are they important? How can we actually *use* these rays? Let me give you an example of how the study of the Seven Rays has impacted my life.

My Story

When I arrived at my first Seven Rays class at Emmabelle's home in 1991, Robbie (Emmabelle's assistant), greeted me at the door. She escorted me into the house, while excitedly summoning Emmabelle and exclaiming, "Look! We have a Ray Two body in our class! We have never seen one before!" I had no idea what they were talking about, while they commented on my tiny wrists and feet and delicate features. I had never had anyone notice me in this way before or get joyous over wrists and feet!

This evening forever changed the relationship I had with myself and the way I viewed my body. Until this dramatic moment, I had always felt "inferior" in terms of my physical body's strength and endurance. I was very small, delicate, fragile, and sensitive. It seemed

I could not keep up with most other people in terms of athletics or endurance. I could not get away with the abuse of the body that others could. I got sick easily and needed much peace and quiet and not too much over-stimulation. This, of course, provoked comments from others, such as, "You're just too sensitive. You need to get thicker skin. Why don't you take better care of yourself so you don't get sick." These reactions from other people who did not appear to have the same physical structure or sensitivity led me to believe that I needed to try to keep up with them and attempt to do what their bodies could do because they were "right" and I was "wrong."

During this most auspicious class, Emmabelle explained to me the phenomenon of the Ray Two physical body. "Most Americans are of the Ray Three physical body. What they do would *kill* you," she laughed as she turned to me. "Ray Two bodies are rare, and most of them are in the Orient," she smiled. That explained my whole life to me, and I suddenly knew that *I really am different.* I knew instinctively that I was different; that was not hard to figure out. I just did not understand *why.* Now I had some real reasons, and I accepted my Ray Two physical body with love. I would no longer "beat myself up" in my mind for being different. I would just relish in the knowledge that I am fine the way I am and that it is okay to be different! I cannot tell you how freeing and healing this information was for me. It was like finding the instructions that came with my body forty-eight years after my birth. I now know that I am special, gifted, and aware, not physically flawed. My rays are just right for this incarnation and my path.

It is fascinating to see the *combination* of rays within an individual person and how they interact. For example, my personal rays are as follows:

Ray Two Physical Body
Ray Two Emotional Body/Changed from Ray Six
Ray Four Mental Body
Ray One Personality
Ray Two Soul
Ray Two Monad

There are four Ray Two's here. Ray Two is receptive, loving, wise, and tends to lean more toward the passive side of life. It also shows gifts of organization, study, patience, and a predilection towards caution, perhaps not moving as quickly into action as a Ray One does, for example. To balance this, I have a Ray One personality, which shows strong leadership, will and power. Ray One makes up for any lack of energy or action that the Ray Two might exhibit. The Ray One personality gets all that love and wisdom out into the world and sets it into action! The Ray Four mental body gives me excellent teaching and communication skills, as does the Ray Two soul. The Ray Four aspect also infuses much perfectionism and some compulsion into my life. Interestingly enough, I started out in this incarnation with a Ray Six emotional body and changed it over to a Ray Two emotional body in the past nine years. This change occurred with the soul-infusion of the personality. It takes hundreds of lifetimes to change the emotional body ray.

With the above information, my life makes a great deal of sense to me. I am a teacher, leader, executive, writer, speaker and healer. The unique combination of strength and sensitivity has given me much compassion and awareness in helping others learn to love themselves as they are and to heal their lives. I see my life with its polarity, vulnerability, and challenges as a gift. All aspects of myself are good, and I see how they all work together to make me the special being that I am. The Ray Analysis has shown me the beauty of graciously accepting myself and understanding the gifts of my life rather than lamenting any perceived appearances of weakness or inferiority. **I am able to lovingly laugh at myself without devaluing myself in any way for any reason.** The study of the Seven Rays has made this possible for me. I have learned to enjoy being who I am instead of trying to be like someone else who has different ray numbers and a different path. Each person has just the right combination of rays to follow his/her path in life. We must celebrate all paths and all our rays to realize the full beauty of our lives.

To further illustrate the value of the Seven Rays knowledge in my life, I ask the following questions: What if I had *not* been born into a sensitive Ray Two body and possessed a sturdier Ray Three body? What if I had not ever been sick or sensitive? Would I possess the compassion or awareness that I have to offer those beautiful souls who I am helping in my daily work as a life coach, counselor, teacher, and healer? I think not. With a different physical body ray, I might have chosen a different career or a different focus on my career, attracting different kinds of experiences and people into my life. As a very important spiritual advisor in my life once pointed out to me, sensitivity means greater awareness. Awareness is a gift that paves the way for visionaries and enlightenment. All is not what it appears to be. Everything has a purpose, a reason for being. Even that which appears to be negative is valuable.

Notes

Chapter 15

The Importance of Ray Combinations

We must also be aware that it is not just the *separate* rays in each person's ray analysis that we need to look at. We need to look at the *combinations* of these rays and how they interact. This is the beauty of the Seven Rays: *By looking at our separate rays and their special combination, we are able to see our gifts, strengths, challenges, vulnerabilities, and the way we approach life. Our ray numbers influence the "way we approach life" in a major way.*

It is important to note that in our journey to enlightenment, self-mastery, and ascension, we must master **all** of the attributes of the Creator— all of the highest aspects of the Seven Rays. We do this by choosing different rays in different incarnations. Therefore, all incarnations and experiences are important! Rather than comparing ourselves to others, we should realize that everyone must eventually master everything. If we are experiencing a difficult life and envying people who "appear" to have a better life, we must remember that this could be reversed in the next incarnation!

Notes

Chapter 16

Putting It All Together

Each person is a combination of six different individual rays: physical, emotional, mental, personality, soul, and monad. Discovering what these particular rays are and learning how to use them effectively throughout your life will bring you more self-awareness, focus and understanding of yourself and your mission.

In order for the knowledge of these rays to be useful to you, you must ascertain your stage in the development ladder of life. According to Zachary F. Lansdowne in *The Rays and Esoteric Psychology*, the stages of evolution for a human being can be described as follows:[17]

1. **Sensual**—the time of infancy when we are polarized in our physical bodies without any intelligent understanding of our environment.

2. **Emotional**—the time of childhood—a time of emotional extremes when children's minds are not sufficiently developed to establish balance or equilibrium.

3. **Mental**—the time of adolescence when the mental consciousness is intelligent, inquiring and intellectually sensitive. However,

the personality is not yet coordinated. The mental focus may alternate with the emotional and sensual extremes.

4. **Ambition**—Young adults develop a sense of responsibility to family members and feel important by regarding others as being dependent. They become ambitious and long for influence and power in some field of endeavor.

5. **Coordination**—Owing to ambition, average adults learn to coordinate the energies of personality, so that the brain and the mind function synchronously. The emotional nature is subordinated, and there is a steady growth in the power to use thought.

6. **Selfish influence**—Advanced adults attain the power to influence, sway, guide and hold others within their range of purpose and desire. Since the higher issues are not yet understood, this power is selfishly used and is frequently destructive.

7. **Group Awareness**—This stage occurs when the aspirants seek to be soul-centered and controlled. They steadily develop group consciousness, or inclusive love, while preserving their self-consciousness and sense of individuality.

In the first five stages of the above list, the individuals are learning how to function as coordinated personalities. During these stages, they are basically self-centered, which is a necessary step on the way to higher consciousness. When the sixth stage is reached, their personalities are coordinated; their characteristics include dominance, ambition, pride, and lack of inclusive love, although they may possess love for those whom they feel are necessary for their comfort. During the seventh stage, they begin to express selflessness, group service and inclusive love.[18]

During the sixth stage of *selfish influence*, a crisis of evocation usually occurs, marking the end of that stage and the beginning of group awareness. People experiencing the *crisis of evocation* find their lives "falling apart" in many ways. This breaking down of the old patterns and belief systems brings them to a new point of awareness and group consciousness. It is at this last stage of group awareness that we can begin to determine the soul ray. As mentioned earlier, it is not until the Third Initiation (mastering of the mental body) that we can contact and realize our monad ray.

To determine which ray is dominant in your life at any time, look at your current stage of life. Then look at your individual ray that corresponds to that stage. The first stage (physical), of course, is the physical body ray. The second stage is the emotional body ray. The third stage is the mental body ray. The fourth, fifth and sixth stages are a composite of the personality ray. The seventh stage brings the soul ray to the forefront.

So we see that different rays dominate at different times of our lives. It is important to remember that *every one of these rays is important and necessary in our development.* We must also remember that each of us must eventually master all of the rays and bring all of their attributes into our essence through multiple lives and ray experiences. Therefore, we should not label or limit ourselves to only the rays that we are currently expressing or are in our "ray chart." *We can call in any ray at any time to balance us or aid us in our lives.*

To summarize, you can determine your ray structure by looking at your current stage of life, your physical, emotional, mental, and personality characteristics, your career choices, your hobbies and special interests, your approach to life, and life experiences. In addition, you can ask for the ray numbers to be revealed to you during meditation, ask for divine guidance, and consult a pendulum if you are proficient and comfortable with that mode. Many people will eventually realize their particular rays through their intuition after looking at all of the above clues. If you would like a "Ray Reading,' I would be delighted to do this for you. Please contact me at my email address for more information.

Use the ray knowledge to pursue the highest expression of each ray's attributes with balance and harmony. I believe that the study of the rays is one of the best tools for self-understanding available to humanity.

Notes

Part Two

Chapter 17

Introduction to Part Two

In Part One of this book, I have discussed the specific qualities of the twelve rays and how they impact our lives. I would now like to create for my readers a *Guidance Manual for Self-Help* in using this information. I hope this guidebook will assist you in:

1. integrating and more fully enjoying your lives
2. creating insight and understanding
3. fulfilling your destiny
4. living to your potential
5. helping you move to the next stage of your development.

The following series of *questions, activities, and guided imagery* will help you determine and integrate your individual rays. This portion will aid you in identifying your talents, vulnerabilities, mission, approach to life, special techniques, possible dangers and challenges, and the focus of the lens through which you view your present life. It will guide you through *various ways that you can use each of the twelve rays to balance, harmonize, and strengthen yourself* on a daily basis as well as impact your whole life in the best way possible.

It is essential to know your ray structure on as many levels as possible in order to make the greatest progress in your spiritual development.

Chapter 18

Ray Proportions in Your Life

The Seven Rays Quiz

Put a check mark before each of the following characteristics that describe you. Then list them in priority from the most important (to you) to the least important on the right side of the listed quality.

_____Ritual   _____
_____Power   _____
_____Love   _____
_____Beauty   _____
_____Organization   _____
_____Action   _____
_____Wisdom   _____
_____Order   _____
_____Idealism   _____
_____Logic   _____
_____Protocol   _____
_____Will   _____
_____Receptivity   _____

_____Dedication   _____
_____Focus   _____
_____Facts   _____
_____Religion   _____
_____Science   _____
_____Art   _____
_____Philosophy   _____
_____Harmony   _____

Interpreting Your Answers

Look at your answers from the preceding quiz. Then check the corresponding rays with the qualities and characteristics that describe you.

Characteristic:	Ray
Ritual	Seven
Power	One
Love	Two
Beauty	Four
Organization	Three
Action	Three
Wisdom	Two
Order	Seven
Idealism	Six
Logic	Five
Protocol	Seven
Will	One
Receptivity	Two
Dedication	Six
Focus	One
Facts	Five
Religion	Six
Science	Five
Art	Four
Philosophy	Three
Harmony	Four

Number of Ray One answers: _____
Number of Ray Two answers: _____
Number of Ray Three answers: _____
Number of Ray Four answers: _____
Number of Ray Five answers: _____
Number of Ray Six answers: _____
Number of Ray Seven answers: _____

List the qualities that you ranked in order of importance on the first page of this quiz and their corresponding ray. List the most important quality first and the least important quality last. Which rays seem to predominate in terms of importance to you?

Chapter 19

Daily Ray Analysis

Each of the Seven Rays is associated with a particular day of the week. They are as follows:

Ray One: Sunday (Red)
Ray Two: Monday (Blue)
Ray Three: Tuesday (Yellow)
Ray Four: Wednesday (Green)
Ray Five: Thursday (Orange)
Ray Six: Friday (Indigo)
Ray Seven: Saturday (Violet)

Look at the day of the week and its corresponding color. You may choose to wear that color, or you may need to balance it out with the color of a different ray. Consciously invoke the highest aspects of that particular ray and color.

Next, look at the colors of your individual rays: physical body ray, emotional body ray, mental body ray, soul ray, and monad ray (if you know it). You may fill in that information here if you know it.

My physical body ray **number** is_____.
My physical body ray **color** is_____.
My emotional body ray **number** is_____.
My emotional body ray **color** is_____.
My mental body ray **number** is_____.
My mental body ray **color** is_____.
My soul ray **number** is_____.
My soul ray **color** is_____.
My monad ray **number** is_____.
My monad ray **color** is_____.

If you have a ray number in your chart that correspond to the color of the day, the attributes and challenges of that ray are intensified for you on that day. This is a powerful day for you, and you will probably be more energized and charged or more passive and tired, more emotional, more objective, etc. For example, if you have a lot of Ray Two in your chart, your Ray Two qualities will be intensified on Mondays. If you have some Ray One in your chart, you may be demonstrating more Ray One qualities on Sundays. For each day of the week, there is a ray that is predominant. Knowing the higher and lower aspects of all of the rays can help you bring in the highest aspect of any ray in a balanced way.

If you find that you are overly charged with a certain ray, you can balance it out with a ray of different quality. The following stories illustrate how this principle worked for one of my clients.

Rachel's Stories

It was a typical Tuesday morning. I was not particularly looking forward to another uneventful day at my job. I felt I needed some motivation. I remembered that in my previous ascension class, we had discussed the various rays in detail. Ray One was described as the ray of will and power. We later were instructed that at any time we could whisper, shout, or even imagine bringing in the quality of a chosen ray.

I decided that on this boring Tuesday Ray One would help my dilemma by providing motivation. I mentally called for the energy of Ray One. Next, I silently prayed and thanked the Creator for this gift. Suddenly, I felt a powerful surge of adrenaline shoot through my body. My heart was beating rapidly as if something had frightened me. This was odd because just seconds before that I was peacefully meditating. The sensation did not leave, so I placed my hand on my heart. Thank goodness, I intuitively thought of Ray Two, the ray of love and wisdom, as a possible counter-balance of Ray One energy.

Immediately after I thought of Ray Two, my heartbeat slowed down. Within seconds, I was able to continue my day with a feeling of balance.

On another occasion, I felt unbalanced and "out of sync." I called in Ray Eight to balance and cleanse my four bodies (physical, emotional, mental, spiritual). As a result, I experienced the best work week I ever had!

Chapter 20

Daily Questions to Ask Yourself

Sample Worksheet

Note: I have included a blank worksheet of these questions following this sample workheet for your convenience.

What color do I choose to wear today?_____
     example: red
What is the ray number for this color?_____
     example: Ray One
How much of this color do I need?_____
     example: a small amount—a red stone or accent
What is my energy level today?_____
     example: low
What color and ray will help balance it?_____
     example: red (Ray One)
What is my "mood" today?_____
     example: quiet, forceful, restful, angry, confident, afraid, insecure
What ray number and color will balance my mood?_____
     example: if angry, bring in Ray Two (blue) for love and compassion

Which of my "bodies" (physical, emotional, mental, soul) is dominating my attention today?_____

example: emotional body

What are the number and color of that ray?_____

example: Ray Six—indigo or Ray Four—green

Which archetype is in charge today?_____

example: organizer

What color will help balance and show that quality today?_____

example: yellow—Ray Three

What qualities to I want to display today?_____

example: professional, businesslike

What are the corresponding rays and colors?_____

example: Ray Three—Yellow, Ray Seven—Violet

How do I want others to see me today?_____

example: Compassionate and Loving

What are the corresponding colors?_____

example: Ray Two—Blue

If you ask yourself these questions daily, you can bring in the "missing" qualities by calling in those particular rays and using the colors of those rays. The color will add its ray; invoking (asking) for that ray will balance and harmonize your four-body system into an integrated personality.

Blank Worksheet

What color do I choose to wear today?_____

What is the ray number for this color?_____

How much of this color do I need?_____

What is my energy level today?_____

What color and ray will help balance it?_____

What is my "mood" today?_____

What ray number and color will balance my mood?_____

Which of my "bodies" (physical, emotional, mental, soul) is dominating my attention today?_____

What are the number and color of that ray?_____

Which archetype is in charge today?_____

What color will help balance and show that quality today?_____

What qualities to I want to display today?_____

What are the corresponding rays and colors?_____

How do I want others to see me today?_____

What are the corresponding colors?_____

Chapter 21

Awareness Journal

In your journal or in this book, write out your answers to the following questions. Keep in mind that there are no wrong answers. Just write what describes the *real* you. Be totally honest.

1. What numbers and colors am I attracted to, like, or see frequently?

2. If I am totally free from "shoulds" and am left to my own devices, what would I like to do the most?

3. What do I like about myself? (physically, emotionally, mentally, spiritually)?

4. What would I like to change about myself? (physically, emotionally, mentally, spiritually)?

5. Describe your physical body.

6. Describe your emotional tendencies. Include patterns, general feelings, forms of expression/repression, etc. Tell about your beliefs about emotions in general and your reactions to your emotions. What is your most dominant emotion? (e.g. anger, fear, worry, pretense, sadness, joy, peace, etc.)

7. Write about your personality traits.

8. I believe my divine mission in life is_____

9. Why?

10. Write a summary and general description of your work history. Tell about your careers (past, present, and dreams for future careers).

11. Write about your hobbies, interests, avocations and recreational activities. Do you see any patterns? Are they related to your work or are they different from your career?

12. Use this page to draw yourself as "light" and "color." How do you look? What colors are you? What shapes are you? Do the colors blend together or are they clearly defined and separated? Color yourself daily on a separate sheet of paper, and note the variations on different days.

13. Write a biographical sketch of your life. See how it pertains to the twelve rays and your particular ray structure. How do the rays interact and shape who you are? What makes you unique?

14. After writing your biographical sketch, answer the following questions:

Which did I emphasize the most—my physical body, my emotional reactions, my mental processes, or my spiritual focus?

*Which of the above did I **not** focus much attention on?*

Where does my perspective come from? Is it emotionally based, physically based, mentally based, or spiritually based?

Is my focus evenly distributed between these four areas?

Draw a circle and fill in the pieces of the pie according to the amount of physical focus, emotional focus, mental focus, spiritual focus. Show percentage rates for each, totaling 100 percent.

15. Use this page to draw the twelve rays as you see them.

Chapter 22

The Seventh Ray

The percentage of rays on our planet is constantly changing. Currently, Rays One, Seven and Twelve are coming in at the fastest rate. *Ray Seven* has a special quality—the *violet flame of transmutation*—that is so important that it must be discussed separately.

According to Ronna Herman's channeling of Archangel Michael in the I AM Mastery Course, Lesson One:

> *"The seventh ray is the activity or power used to etherialize. It is used on other planets to transmute and turn the substance of anything that has fulfilled its service and is of no further use back to the universe. This includes physical bodies at the end of a lifetime, a life of service. Etherialization is simply releasing the electrons back into the unformed ready to be used again.*
>
> *The violet flame is used in all higher realms. It is used by Divine and Ascended Beings to etherialize whatever has come forth or has been drawn forth in any realm that was not utilized, as well as all that which has been utilized and has completed its service, thereby returning the substance back into the realm for re-use. Life is very conservative. This ray is also the action to invoke and magnetize and radiate. This is*

> its use on other planets where it is not required for purifica-
> tion. Its activity is to draw the sacred fire through the power
> of invocation, through thought, feeling and the spoken word.
> The Three-fold Flame is the magnet within the individual
> that draws primal life force from its source…God.
>
> It is known that rapid vibrations rise. They are drawn to
> the Realm of Light where the frequency is rapid, while the
> slower or heavier realm vibrations descend or sink and stay
> in the atmosphere of the Earth. That is why the perfection
> from the Realms of Light must be drawn down here.
>
> In order to do that, there must be a magnetic center, a
> magnetization by which it is drawn and then radiated out.
> This is done through the individual and through groups. It is
> the service of the Seventh Ray."[19]

The Seventh Ray Violet Flame of transmutation is powerful in its ability to transform any form of negativity into purified Divine Light substance. Thus, the energy that was being used in sustaining that negativity is now freed up and returned to you purified. This "negative energy" can take the form of conflict from within and without, trauma, unpleasant memories, obsessions/compulsions, relationships, financial problems, faulty, critical and judgmental thinking, past and present mistakes, fear, perceived problems in the future, the negative emotions of anger, rage, fear, worry, pretense, grief, sadness, perceived "attack" from others or towards others, etc. With an awareness of the power of the Violet Flame, all you need to do is to call in the Violet Fame to transmute whatever you do not wish to continue experiencing or remembering. The Violet Flame can be used in meditation for a general clearing process; it can also be invoked in specific situations for cleansing and clearing.

The energy of the seventh ray has a way of aiding you in your understanding and elevating your level of insight in situations. For example, if you call in the seventh ray and the Violet Flame of transmutation, you may be able to see clearly what you could not see before. The clarity of the situation now shows you what needs to be done next. This is an incredibly powerful tool in cleansing, purification and soul growth. Using the Violet Flame can help you to understand yourself more completely and to unlock and go beyond that understanding. It brings you to a higher and more harmonious level.[20]

You can use the Violet Flame in meditations and send it out to the entire Earth, visualizing the Earth being cleansed and transmuted. This is a very specific and effective tool in planetary healing. You are not a powerless victim—you can always send out the Violet Flame to anywhere on the planet or use it within yourself.

With the knowledge of the seventh ray Violet Flame of transmutation, our world has incredible possibilities of instantaneous healing. Think of the implications of its use in therapy. If, for example, a person is seeing a psychiatrist or counselor to solve some problems, the Violet Flame could save many years of gut-wrenching analysis, suffering, being "stuck," and the reliving of painful memories and traumas. All too often, the trauma is not released even after such a grueling process, to which many people can attest. This is because the terrible emotional and/or physical suffering prevents the patient's willingness to let go, forgive and forget, move on, change behaviors, and see possibilities for the future without this encumbrance.

Bringing in the Violet Flame can help to clear and cleanse the negative energy of the past, elevate the patient to a higher and more harmonious level where he or she is now able to see with clarity what needs to be done. The Violet Flame has unlocked the patient from the grasp of the trauma, freed him to see objectively with new understanding and to walk away from the wreckage with healing and wholeness. I am not saying that counseling is not necessary. I believe that it is a highly effective tool. The Violet Flame can greatly enhance the healing process and shorten the length of time it takes.

Now let's look at the possibilities *planetarily*. If we visualize the Violet Flame in political hot spots, potential or actual war zones, or any area where there is strife and suffering, we can help to actually transmute this negativity, clear and cleanse the situation, and lift the area to a higher level where healing becomes possible. This can be done in an instant—for that is all it takes to call in the Violet Flame! We are no longer bound by the constraints of time and the slowness built in to the old processes.

Many people may find the concept of the Violet Flame hard to believe because it sounds too simplistic and possibly even ridiculous. Our past programming has taught that solutions only come through long, drawn-out and complicated processes. We have "bought into" the concept of high technology, expensive equipment, terminal bureaucracy and limitation. We can compare the Violet Flame to microwave ovens. Before they were commonplace, the idea of cooking a meal in minutes that normally would take hours seemed preposterous. The Violet Flame speeds up the healing process just as the microwave oven speeds up the cooking process! If you are a "doubting Thomas," meditate on the Violet Flame and bring it into your challenges. Pay attention to the outcome. I think you will notice some miracles!

Chapter 23

Glamours and Pitfalls

All of the Rays have higher aspects and lower aspects. There are also certain traps that we can fall into. These traps are called "glamours and pitfalls" because they represent the negative patterns of thought and action that may actually have seductive appeal for us. While we are entrenched in any negative pattern, we are blind to its illusion and can become very unbalanced. We are susceptible to the glamours of our particular rays. Briefly, they are as follows:

Ray One Glamours

Ray One is the ray of power, will and purpose. Ray One "pitfalls" include:

> the love of power and authority
> pride
> selfish ambition
> impatience
> self-centeredness
> aloofness
> separateness

To balance the love of power, transform it into the love of *service*. A first-ray being needs to incorporate the second-ray qualities of love and wisdom. First-ray people need to work on developing:

tenderness
compassion
humility
sympathy
tolerance
patience.

To avoid the glamours of Ray One, *meditate and seek attunement with God.* Take the higher path, not the lower. Visualizing the colors of blue and pink (second ray) is also helpful.

Ray Two Glamours

Ray Two is the ray of Love/Wisdom. The pitfalls of Ray Two are:

Fear
Negativity
A sense of inferiority and inadequacy
Depression
Constant anxiety
Self-pity
Inertia
Ineffectiveness

To balance these pitfalls, invoke the opposite qualities. Cultivate joy, a positive attitude, courage and strength. Affirm the positive, and do not give any energy to the negative side of this ray.

It is also very helpful to call in the ninth ray, which is the ray of joy, to heal depression. Visualize blue-green (the color of the ninth ray).

Calling in the seventh-ray Violet Flame of transmutation is a very powerful way of transmuting that which is undesirable, misqualified, or negative into purified Divine Light substance.

Invoking a small amount of Ray One energy for more power, strength and will is sometimes a good balancer for Ray Two pitfalls. Visualize a small amount of red energy.

Another helpful way to balance the negative side of Ray Two is to invoke Ray Five and visualize the color orange.

Ray Three Glamours

Ray Three is the ray of active, creative intelligence. The glamours and pitfalls of Ray Three are as follows:

Always being busy
Being preoccupied with detail
Materialism
Scheming and manipulating others
Self-interest
Deviousness
Self-importance in being the "one who knows"
Intellectual pride
Coldness
Isolation
Inaccuracy in details
Absent-mindedness
Obstinacy
Too much criticism of others

If the above vices are a problem, temper this ray with the love and wisdom of Ray Two and the devotion of Ray Six. Call in the blue second ray color/energy and the indigo Ray Six color/energy.

Stay attuned to God and the Higher Self, not corruption. It is always helpful to invoke the opposite qualities if the negative side of the ray is a problem. Call forth the attributes of perseverance, manifestation, organization, and mental illumination. Center yourself spiritually, and always ask for the manifestation of that which is the highest and best for all concerned.

Ray Four Glamours

Ray Four is the ray of harmony through conflict, beauty, and art. The pitfalls and glamours of Ray Four are:

> Constant inner and outer conflict
> Manipulation of others
> Causing arguments and trouble
> Over-sensitivity and dissatisfaction with life
> Being impractical
> Lack of focus and continuity, changing all the time
> Diffusion of interest and energy
> Tendency toward manic-depression
> Glamour of imagination
> Being a victim
> Being overly-emotional

To balance the negative sides of Ray Four, it is essential that you meditate and develop spiritual awareness and focus. Stay centered in your spiritual self. Seek balance and work on not falling victim to all of the glamours and your emotions. This is a very sensitive ray. Invoke the qualities of balance, peace, serenity, will, purpose, self-control, mental and moral balance, confidence and grounding. It is essential that Ray Four people balance their dreamy visions and artistic talents by staying grounded. It is absolutely essential that they balance their emotions.

Invoking the first-ray is very helpful for Ray Four balance. Ask Archangel Michael for protection and strength.

Calling forth Rays Three and Five is very effective in balancing the negative side of Ray Four.

Ray Five Glamours

Ray Five is the ray of concrete science and knowledge. The glamours and pitfalls of Ray Five are:

Being stuck in the mental body
Not allowing intuition and connection with the soul
Being pedantic
Becoming too focused on trivial details
Hair-splitting and harsh criticism
Narrow-mindedness
Arrogance
Lack of sympathy and reverence
Prejudice
Unforgiving temper
Over-emphasis on form
Intellectual pride
Lack of feeling
Too much mental detachment

To balance the above vices of Ray Five, call in the love and wisdom of Ray Two, a very small amount of the highest aspects of Ray Four, and/or the devotion of Ray Six. Of course, it is always good to cultivate the qualities of love, wisdom, beauty, harmony, devotion, reverence, sympathy, and open-mindedness. Mediate and stay attuned to God and what is the highest and best for all concerned. A good mantra for this is: "May the blessings be for the good of the whole."

Ray Six Glamours

Ray Six is the Ray of Devotion and Idealism. The glamours and pitfalls of Ray Six are:

Fanaticism
Possessiveness
Love of the past and existing forms

Rigidity
Over-emotionalism
Narrow-mindedness
Bigotry
Seeing things as either perfect or intolerable
Over-devotion and excessive religious fervor

To balance this highly emotional ray, call forth the aspects of clarity, emotional balance, discretion, broad-mindedness, moderation, detachment, impersonal and unconditional love, letting go of the past and moving forward, adaptation to change, and flexibility,

Calling in the highest aspects of Rays One, Three, Five and Seven will help balance Ray Six over-zealousness. These rays will provide objectivity, dilute the over-emotionalism of Ray Six. Mental energy has a healing effect on too much intensity. Meditation and attunement to God and the highest spiritual path of life will greatly assuage the pitfalls of Ray Six and, of course, all of the rays.

Ray Seven Glamours

Ray Seven is the ray of Ceremonial Order and Magic. The glamours of this ray are as follows:

Superstition
Excessive interest in omens, dreams and spiritual phenomena
Formalism
Bigotry
Pride
Superficial judgments
Narrowness
Over-indulgence
Rigid adherence to law and order
Over-emphasis on organization
Love of the secret and mysterious sides of life
Glamour of ceremony and ritual
Overemphasis of inappropriate psychic and occult ceremonies

Calling in the seventh-ray Violet Flame of transmutation is a very effective way of transmuting negativity into pure Divine Light substance. Cultivate the qualities of strength, perseverance, self-reliance, extreme care in details, and courtesy. Meditate on these qualities to create a healthy integration of Ray Seven. Stay attuned to God and work for the highest good of all.

Call in the second ray of love and wisdom for balance. Visualize the color of blue for wisdom and pink for love. Pray for the manifestation of the highest aspects of Ray Seven.

General Guidelines

Here are some general guidelines in dealing with the glamours and pitfalls of all of the rays:

1) Call forth the opposite, positive qualities.
2) Invoke the highest aspects of other rays for balance.
3) Stay spiritually centered.
4) Meditate.
5) Be aware of what qualities you are projecting. Do a character analysis and self-inventory to see what needs to change.
6) Call on masters and archangels of the rays for assistance. (See page 100.)

There are many wonderful gifts and talents associated with each of the rays. It is important that we do not fall into the pitfalls and glamours of each ray—especially the second ray, of which we are all a part. (We are all on a sub-ray of Ray Two because the solar system is of Ray Two.) We also might still be reacting to special rays from previous incarnations and carrying the lower or negative aspects of these rays. We must purify ourselves and deeply cleanse ourselves of any imbalances or tendencies towards the lower aspects of each ray. This is of utmost importance for the splendor of God to lift us to our divine essence.

In order to be truly balanced, we must balance the physical, emotional, mental and spiritual bodies. Ignoring your physical body, emotions, and mind and only focusing on your spiritual growth is another trap that must be avoided at all costs. We must have all aspects of ourselves—our physical body, emotions, mind, psychological development, human relationships, groundedness, ability to function as independent adults in the material world, philosophical beliefs, etc.—in place and balanced if we are to become whole and effective and achieve our divine mission on Earth.

Notes

Chapter 24

Balancing the Rays

The following is a chart of how to offset any imbalances in the rays. If you are experiencing any negative aspects of a ray or too much of a particular ray, you can offset these imbalances by calling in other rays for balance. Ray Seven may be used to balance *all of the rays* by invoking the seventh ray violet flame of transmutation.

To offset:	Use:
Ray One	Ray Two Ray Seven
Ray Two	Ray Nine Ray Seven
Ray Three	Ray Two a small amount of Ray Six Ray Seven

Ray Four ....Ray One
                       Ray Three
                       Ray Five
                       Ray Seven

Ray Five ....Ray Four
                       Ray Two
                       Ray Six
                       Ray Seven

Ray Six ....Ray One
                       Ray Three
                       Ray Five
                       Ray Seven

Ray Seven ....Ray Two

Chapter 25

Archangels and Masters

The twelve rays are not affiliated with any religion, cult, or particular belief system. The rays are the energetic and vibrational substances that constitute all matter. Just as people are composed of atoms, molecules, electrons, etc., so is everything in creation, including plants, minerals, rocks, planets, humans, animals, the nature kingdom and all life, made up of rays. The rays are the attributes and qualities of the Undifferentiated Source or the Absolute all-inclusive Whole, and all creations are composed of rays. These energies and forces are essentially neutral and depend on their effectiveness for good or bad on the spiritual development of a person, nation, or humanity as a whole. We respond according to the state of our own development in consciousness.[21]

Behind each ray stands a great Cosmic Being who is in charge of that particular ray—a Department Head, so to speak. These "Department Heads" are not to be worshipped, but rather to be called on for assistance, since they are experts on that particular ray. Each human being belongs by nature to a particular ray but will also include the other six ray types. There is nothing in the whole solar system at whatever stage of evolution it may stand, which does not belong and has not always belonged to one or other of the Seven Rays.[22]

These great Cosmic Beings or "department heads" are also assisted by Archangels and ascended masters who help to dispense or infuse the rays to created life. They are not to be worshipped, and they do not correlate to any particular religious belief system. Rather, they are experts in their field and are available to assist us. We can call on these great Cosmic Beings of Light at any time to assist us in bringing in a particular ray and its highest qualities.

Some people may have difficulty understanding the terminology of "Archangels" and "masters." I would like to emphasize again that the Twelve Rays have nothing to do with religion or individual spiritual beliefs. They are the substance of life without individualization. People and separate life forms individualize the rays to create their own unique combination of traits, qualities, characteristics, beliefs, and behaviors. The rays are neutral.

When we bring in a discussion of Archangels and masters, we are only referring to Specialists who are here to serve us. Please do not confuse these Archangels and masters with any particular religious beliefs. They transcend religion. They are spiritually available for all sentient beings of every religion and belief system.

Angels have appeared throughout the known history of this planet. They have been recognized by the major world religions, and they have been personally experienced by many as guardian angels. These guardian angels have been perceived as being both the givers of protection and inspiration. The Archangels are the major angels who are in charge of all others and serve on different rays—the Department Heads and managers.

To illustrate how religion relates to the rays, religion is a quality of Ray Six, the Ray of Devotion and Idealism. All religions – their use and misuse—fall under Ray Six. The rays are all-inclusive and encompass no defined belief system.

The following table shows the various Rays and the Masters, Archaii and Archangels who are available to assist us with the Rays.

RAY	ARCHANGEL	ARCHAII	MASTERS
One	Michael	Lady Faith	El Morya
Two	Jophiel	Lady Constance	Kuthumi
Three	Chamuel	Lady Clarity	Serapis Bey
Four	Gabriel	Lady Hope	Paul the Venetian
Five	Raphael	Lady Mary	Hilarion
Six	Uriel	Lady Grace	Sananda
Seven	Zadkiel	Lady Amethyst	St. Germain

(Rays Eight, Nine, Ten, Eleven, and Twelve are combinations of the first seven rays)

Notes

Chapter 26

Interacting With Other Rays

Every person is a complex individual with a unique ray structure. Learning your own rays is of great value in living your life to its fullest potential. It is also very beneficial, if not essential, to learn how to interact with people on the other rays. In order to do this, you need to understand the nature of all of the rays and how to communicate with them.

I would like to give you a very brief outline of how to communicate with the various rays in business, social situations and in general.

Interacting with Ray One

Be confident and strong. Show a sense of purpose, motivation and focus on a goal. Have a step-by-step plan to achieve your goals.

Interacting with Ray Two

Show that you care. Ask about how their family is doing and how they are feeling. Concentrate on concepts and human relationships in a loving and wise manner.

Interacting with Ray Three

Be organized, orderly, and persistent. Concentrate on philosophy and action. Stay focused and organized. Outline the steps to get the job done.

Interacting with Ray Four

Appeal to the person's sense of harmony and beauty. Focus on serenity and balance. Show flexibility and sensitivity to their views and needs. Be appreciative of their talents. Allow them to express themselves.

Interacting with Ray Five

Be ready to present the facts with accuracy and proof. Show statistics, and be sure to have all your "ducks in a row." Be objective and adaptable.

Interacting with Ray Six

Show human interest and emphasize "one-on-one" relationships and communication. Show dedication and emphasize the philosophical aspects of the situation. Use personal examples; it is permissible to be "flowery" at times.

Interacting with Ray Seven

Present yourself well, and look good. Be very organized, well dressed, and respectful with the proper use of protocol.

Chapter 27

The Ray Shapes

The following information is channeled from Djwahl Khul:

We can illustrate the Seven Rays with the following geometric shapes:

Ray One	Straight Line	focused intent straight to the goal
Ray Two	Circle	all-encompassing
Ray Three	Staircase	organized, persistent
Ray Four	Rolling Curve	Hills and valleys
Ray Five	Connected Squares	Orderly, scientific
Ray Six	Cross or Plus Sign	Dedication, Idealism
Ray Seven	Crown, Flame	Ceremonial Magic Violet Flame

Chapter 28

Invocations for the Rays

There are many ways to invoke the twelve rays. You may simply ask for any specific ray(s) by their number, color, or qualities. You can also call on the Archangels or masters that correspond to each ray. You do not need to worry about *how* you call on the rays. Simply calling them in will guarantee their arrival to you. When you call on them, they always respond. It is not the *method* that you use that is so important; it is the *intention* that counts.

Here are some suggestions and meditations for calling in the twelve rays.

Invoking Ray One

Divine Will and Power
You may receive Ray One energy in any of the following ways: (Or you can create your own invocation or meditation).

Ask to receive the red energy.

Ask for an infusion of a small amount of Ray One.

Ask for the qualities of divine will, power, and purpose.

Call on Archangel Michael, Lady Faith or El Morya to send you the energy of Ray One to assist you.

Wear the color of the ray. (Red for Ray One)
Imagine the color or the number of the ray.

Ray One Meditation

*Sit or lie in a comfortable position. Close your eyes. Take a few deep breaths
and relax.*

*See in your mind's eye an infusion of a small amount of red energy coming
into your being. This energy is tinged with a small amount of blue. See
Archangel Michael with his sword of power and strength tempered with love
and compassion cutting all negative cords of energy from you within and
without. Breathe in the red energy and feel yourself energized, empowered,
motivated, focused with will, purpose, and power.*

*Take a few minutes to feel this energy and ask Master El Morya and
Archangel Michael to infuse your being with their essence and their knowledge
and wisdom. See if they have any message(s) for you. You may hear this
message in words, or feel it or just absorb it into your being—to be awakened
later for your understanding and insight.*

*Thank Archangel Michael and El Morya for their blessings and gifts. Bless
the Ray One energy within you, vowing to use it only for constructive purposes
for your highest and best good and for the good of the whole.*

*Bring yourself back into the consciousness of your physical body. Send a
grounding cord from your solar plexus into the center of the Earth, and bring
it back up into your first three chakras.*

When you are ready, you may open your eyes.

Invoking Ray Two

Love and Wisdom

To bring in Ray Two, you may do any or all of the following (or you
may create your own invocation).

Ask to receive the blue energy of wisdom.

Ask for the pink energy of love.

Ask for the qualities of love and wisdom.

Call on Ray Two to shower you with its energy.

Call on Archangel Jophiel, Lady Constance and/or Master Kuthumi to assist you.

Wear the color of blue or both pink and blue.

Imagine the color of blue. (You may also imagine pink.)

Imagine the number two.

Ray Two Meditation

Sit or lie in a comfortable position. Close your eyes. Take a few deep breaths and relax.

Feel the color blue coming from above your head down through your head and spine through all of the chakras. Feel this blue color infuse your whole being. Rest in this wonderful color of blue. Imagine a blue thread handing from inside the top of your head down through your spine, balancing and harmonizing your body.

Breathe in this color blue and bathe in its essence of love and wisdom for several minutes. Feel yourself infused with peace, serenity, unconditional love for yourself and all beings.

Ask Archangel Jophiel and Master Kuthumi to infuse your being with their essence and their wisdom and love. Breathe this in for a few minutes. Ask Archangel Jophiel and Master Kuthumi if they have a message for you. Allow this to descend into your being. Thank the masters for their blessings and their gifts of love, compassion, insight, serenity, non-judgment, and knowledge.

When you are ready, gently come back into the awareness of your physical body. Send a grounding cord down into the center of the earth, and bring that cord back up into your body to the navel area. Gently open your eyes.

Invoking Ray Three

Active, Creative Intelligence

To bring in Ray Three, you may do any or all of the following. (You may also create your own invocation.)

Ask to receive the yellow energy.

Call forth Ray Three.

Ask for the qualities of active intelligence and philosophy.

Call on Archangel Chamuel, Lady Clarity and/or Master Serapis Bey to assist you.

Wear yellow.

Imagine yellow and the number three.

Ray Three Meditation

Sit or lie in a comfortable position. Close your eyes. Take a few deep breaths and relax.

Imagine the color of yellow or a golden yellow in the center of your body. This yellow energy is like the sun and is radiating out in all directions. The yellow fills your entire body and aura. Feel the golden glow of love and intelligence flooding your whole being. Bathe in this marvelous yellow radiance. Breathe it in and feel yourself activated with will, intelligent action, adaptability and love of conceptual truth. Feel the warmth of the sun around you and within you.

Take a few minutes to feel this yellow energy. Ask Archangel Chamuel and Master Serapis Bey to fill you with their essence and their special qualities of active intelligence. Ask each of them if they have a special message for you. Breathe deeply while you receive the vibrations of their message. Thank Archangel Chamuel and Master Serapis Bey for their special blessings and gifts.

When you are ready, gently come back into the awareness of your physical body. Send a grounding cord into the center of the earth, and bring it back up to your solar plexus area. Gently open your eyes.

Invoking Ray Four

Harmony, Beauty, and Art

You may create your own method of calling in Ray Four, or you may use any of the following invocations:

Ask to receive the green energy.

Ask for an infusion of Ray Four.

Call forth the qualities of harmony, beauty, and art.

Call on Archangel Gabriel, Lady Hope, and/or Paul the Venetian for assistance.

Wear the color green.
Imagine the color green.
Imagine the number four.

Ray Four Meditation

Sit or lie in a comfortable position. Close your eyes. Take a few deep breaths and relax.

In your mind's eye, bring a beautiful clear green color into your being. Let this green fill your entire body and aura. Feel the soothing, calming, and healing joy of this wonderful green. Bathe in the clear beauty of the green.

Now, see yourself walking in a lush green forest. Everywhere you see varying shades of green—green trees, green plants, green shrubbery, green bushes, and green leaves strewn on the ground. From above a radiant golden light shines on the green, illuminating it with the Light of the Creator.

Breathe this lush green color into your lungs, your heart, your throat, your head, and your entire body. Breathe in the harmony, beauty and art into your being. Bathe in the lovely healing qualities of the green. See the beauty all around you.

Ask Archangel Gabriel, Lady Hope and Paul the Venetian to infuse you with their essence and their beauty and harmony. See if they have any messages for you. You may hear this message in words, or you may feel it or just absorb it vibrationally into your being—to be awakened later for your understanding and insight.

Thank Archangel Gabriel, Lady Hope, and Paul the Venetian for their blessings and gifts. Bless the Ray Four energy within you, vowing to use its highest qualities for the good of all.

Stay in this lush green forest as long as you like. When you are ready, gently bring yourself back into your physical body. Send a grounding cord into the center of the Earth, and bring it back up through your body to your solar plexus.

Open your eyes when you are ready.

Invoking Ray Five

Concrete Science and Knowledge

You may receive Ray Five energy in any of the following ways, or you can create your own invocation or meditation.

Ask to receive the orange energy.

Call forth Ray Five.

Call forth the qualities of concrete science, logic and mathematical precision.

Ask Archangel Raphael, Lady Mary, and/or Hilarion to assist you.

Wear the color orange.

Imagine the color orange.

Imagine the number five.

Ray Five Meditation

Sit or lie in a comfortable position. Close your eyes. Take a few deep breaths, and relax.

Bring in the color orange. See Raphael, Lady Mary and Hilarion sending you orange streams of light and round orange balls of light all around you. These orange streams of light contain unconditional love, pure science and logic, focus and healing properties. Feel yourself lifted up into the higher realms of pure truth and healing. Bask in the orange, and breathe it into your essence.

Now see yourself in a lovely garden. All around you are orange blossoms, orange groves, and an orange sunset. Stroll through this orange garden and feel the freshness and warmth all around you. Bring the orange into every cell, atom, and molecule of your being.

Ask Archangel Raphael, Lady Mary and Hilarion to walk with you in this orange garden and to give you their special messages and gifts. Take a few minutes to feel their blessings and gifts. What are they? Absorb them into your essence. Thank these beings of light for their magnificent assistance.

When you are ready, you may slowly come back into your body, send a grounding cord into the center of the Earth, and open your eyes.

Invoking Ray Six

Abstract Idealism and Devotion

To bring in Ray Six, you may do any of the following, or create your own invocation and meditation.

Call forth Ray Six.

Ask for the indigo energy.

Call forth the qualities of devotion, spiritual nourishment, faith and forgiveness.

Call on Archangel Uriel, Lady Grace and Sananda for assistance.

Wear the color indigo.

Imagine the color indigo.

Imagine the number six.

Ray Six Meditation

Sit or lie in a comfortable position. Close your eyes. Take a few deep breaths and relax.

Imagine a beautiful indigo light all around you and within you. Feel the radiance of this indigo permeating every cell in your body. Bathe in the indigo, and breathe it into your body. See the Archangel Uriel, Lady Grace, and Sananda showering you with the qualities of dedication and devotion, faith, forgiveness, ministering to others in unconditional love, and healing. Thank them for their blessings and gifts. Ask them if they have any messages for you. Take a few minutes to receive these messages.

Now imagine all of the people in your life who would benefit from these qualities that you have now infused into your being. Visualize yourself using the Ray Six qualities in all of your relationships. See all conflicts and problems resolved with unconditional love and healing. Bless all the people in your life, and see them healed. See yourself radiating only unconditional love, forgiveness, and devotion. Breathe in the indigo and absorb it into your essence.

When you are ready, you may slowly return to your physical body, send a grounding cord into the center of the Earth, and open your eyes.

Invoking Ray Seven

Ceremonial Order, Magic, and Ritual

You can bring in Ray Seven in any of the following ways, or you can create your own invocation and meditation.

Call forth Ray Seven.

Ask to receive the violet energy.

Ask for the infusion of the qualities of ceremonial order and magic.

Call in the Violet Transmuting Flame for purification.

Call on Archangel Zadkiel, Lady Amethyst, or St. Germain for assistance.

Wear the color violet.

Imagine the color violet and the number seven.

Ray Seven Meditation

Sit or lie in a comfortable position. Close your eyes. Take a few deep breaths and relax.

In your mind's eye, picture yourself completely immersed in a violet flame. This purple/violet flame now transmutes all negativity within you and around you into pure divine light substance. Bathe in the violet flame and feel yourself becoming free and pure. Feel the violet energy erasing all traumatic experiences of the past and memories, neutralizing all fear, anger, worry, grief, sadness, and pretense. See the violet energy transmuting all unresolved conflicts in all areas of your life—past and present.

As you invite the violet flame to purify you on every level, you are now free and pure to live fully in the present without the burdens and pain of the past. Ask St. Germain, Archangel Zadkiel, and Lady Amethyst if they have a special message or gift for you. Take a few minutes to absorb this into your essence.

Thank these Great Beings of Cosmic Light for their blessings. Vow to keep the image of the Violet Flame around you always—purifying and transmuting all negativity or misqualified energy.

When you are ready, gently come back into your body. Send a grounding cord into the center of the Earth, and open your eyes.

Invoking Ray Eight

Cleansing

Ray Eight is a blend of Ray Four's emotional energy, Ray Seven's physical energy, and Ray Five's mental energy infused with the Light of wholeness and luminosity.

You may receive the energy of Ray Eight in any of the following ways, or you can create your own invocation or meditation.

Ask to receive the luminous green and violet ray.

Ask for an infusion of Ray Eight.

Call forth the qualities of cleansing the four lower bodies.

Call forth the sea-foam green ray.

Call on Lady Nada to fully anchor and activate the Eighth Ray of Higher Cleansing.

Imagine the color sea-foam green and the number eight.

Ray Eight Meditation

Sit or lie in a comfortable position. Close your eyes. Take a few deep breaths and relax.

Call in the Violet Transmuting Flame of the Seventh Ray to transmute all negativity from your four lower bodies into pure divine light substance. Feel your entire four-body system being purified by the violet flame. Bathe in the positive effects of this Violet Transmuting Flame. Allow it to transform you to a higher level of consciousness.

Now call forth the seven ray masters and Djwhal Khul (pronounced "Dwall Cool") to clear all lower and/or negative attributes from the first seven rays and replace them with the higher, positive attributes.

Call forth the beautiful Lady Nada to fully anchor and activate the eighth ray of higher cleansing. See yourself being bathed in this beautiful ray of sea-foam green, a combination of luminous green and violet. Bathe in the positive effects of this cleansing sea-foam green color. Feel the cool, refreshing color purifying your physical body, your emotions, and your mental body. Bask in the lightness and purity as you relax and let go of all negativity and toxins on all levels. You are becoming a crystal—a clear vessel filled with pure sea-foam green cool light. Float in this lovely feeling for as long as you like.

*Bring this green-violet luminosity **very gradually** into the center of your forehead. Do not overdo it; just gently visualize this ray gently on your fore-head for a few seconds.*

Ask if there are any messages that Spirit wishes you to receive.

(You may incorporate the use of a clear quartz crystal placed in the center of the forehead if you wish. You may bring the eighth ray through the crystal.)

Thank Lady Nada and the masters of the seven rays for their help. Bless the Ray Eight energy within you as it continues to cleanse your four lower bodies. Know that you may call on this ray of higher cleansing at any time.

When you are ready, come back into your physical body. Send a grounding cord into the center of the Earth, and open your eyes.

Invoking Ray Nine

Joy

To bring in the energy of Ray Nine, you may do any of the following (or you may create your own invocation).

Ask for the beautiful light green-blue (not quite aqua) energy.

Request an infusion of *joy and light*.

Call on Ray Nine to shower you with its energy.

Call forth the Mother Mary to fully anchor and activate the ninth ray of joy and attracting the Lightbody.

Wear the color of green-blue.

Imagine the number nine and the color of green-blue.

Ray Nine Meditation

Sit or lie in a comfortable position. Close your eyes. Take a few deep breaths and relax.

Visualize a lush green enchanted forest. Everywhere you look you see plush blue-green trees, tall grassy-green shrubbery, and wild flowers of varying shades of blue with green leaves. A clear stream of water meanders along part of the forest, with a blue-green reflection when you look into the water. The gentle bubbling sound of the stream is soothing and musical. Above you is a shaft of golden-white sunlight intersecting the forest like a soft skylight. This luminous white light gives a translucent glow throughout the forest, softening and brightening the blue-green effect, giving it a mint green cast. The cool, harmonizing calm of the varying shades of mint, blue, aqua, and green brings peace and joy to your heart and mind.

Now imagine yourself as a young child of five or six- years old. Picture yourself as a vibrantly healthy and happy youngster playing in this lush green forest. What do you see yourself doing? How do you feel? Are you singing a merry tune and skipping along the path between the mighty trees? Are you laughing with glee and delight at the myriads of tiny life forms beneath your feet? Are you delighting in the feel of the warm sun on your body? Spend several minutes fully enjoying every detail of this joyous experience. How are you dressed? Do you have a pet, a favorite toy, or a friend with you? Be that spontaneous young child, exploring the beauty around you.

Ask the trees and the many life forms in the forest if they have a message for you. Feel the inspiration pouring into your being. You feel the warmth of angelic presence around you, filling you with unconditional love and complete peace. You feel loved, completely protected and safe. You feel total joy. Take plenty of time to fully experience this rapture.

Now picture yourself as your are today in this setting. Bring this joy and peace into your heart. Fill your entire body—every cell, organ, atom, and system with joy and peace and the Light of God. Let this joy expand into your emotions, your mind, and your spirit. Become one with the blue-green of the forest and the joy and the Light of God. Feel totally empowered and confident.

Vow to take this joy, peace, empowerment, and confidence with you always. It is yours forever; you need never relinquish it to anyone or anything. Your joy is locked inside you forever, always with you. If anything in the world ever threatens to disturb your happiness or peace, you can always immediately return to this place of joy within your heart.

Thank the beautiful forest, all of nature, and the angelic beings for this blessed experience. Know that you can always find joy in going beyond yourself into nature whenever your world becomes too stressful.

When you are ready, gently come back into the awareness of your physical body. Send a grounding cord into the center of the earth, and slowly bring that cord back up into your body to the navel area. Gently open your eyes and smile.

Invoking Ray Ten

Coding the Body of Light into the Physical Body

You may receive Ray Ten in any of the following ways, or you may create your own invocation or meditation.

Ask to receive Ray Ten energy.

Ask for the pearlescent energy of Ray Ten.

Call forth the anchoring of your Lightbody into your physical body.

Visualize a pearlescent color and the number ten.

Ray Ten Meditation

Sit or lie in a comfortable position. Close your eyes. Take a few deep breaths and relax.

Imagine that you are at a beautiful pristine beach by the ocean. It is night time, and the moon is shining on the silky white sand and blue water, giving everything—including you—a pearlescent glow. You are lying on the sand alone, looking up at the clear sky and beautiful twinkling stars that seem to be sparkling just for you. There is a slight breeze, but you are not cold. The moisture from the water occasionally sprinkles drops of water on you, which refresh your body and mind. Be there for several minutes and bathe in the clear, cleansing pearlescent moonlight. Feel the sacredness of the moment and allow Spirit to gently whisper in your ear the secrets of the universe.

As you lie on the sandy beach in the moonlight, you feel the pearl-colored luminosity of your Lightbody and the tenth ray energy descending onto you. The light of a thousand suns seems to be shining upon you. You are warm, but not hot. Feel the intensity as you connect with its electrical quality. See in your mind's eye the changes that take place in your body, mind and emotions, your very being. Feel the transformation and elevation to a higher plane as you bathe in this magnificent tenth ray. Allow the divine coding to anchor itself within you, allowing you to grow and merge with your soul and monad.

Flow into the bliss of uniting the physical body with the body of Light, the body of Spirit. All around you is a translucent glow, as you become your Lightbody. Anchor it into your physical being all the way to your toes. Let the pictures in your mind unfold like a movie as you watch the new patterns, geometric codes and transformation take place—like a picture of your future. Allow your pattern of divinity to encode itself within your four-body structure. Stay with this as long as you need to.

Now send this electrical energy of the tenth ray in to the Earth. As you do this, you are bringing your body of Light closer into reality for yourself and for the Earth.

Bless the Creator for shining this tenth ray upon you. Know that you will be forever changed—uplifted in your awareness and manifestation on the Earth plane. Feel the peace of the quiet beach in the moonlight and rest as long as you wish.

When you are ready, come back slowly into your physical body, send a grounding cord in to the center of the Earth, and open your eyes.

Invoking Ray Eleven

Bridge to Higher Consciousness, Service
You may receive Ray Eleven energy in any of the following ways, or you may create your own invocation and/or meditation.
Call forth Ray Eleven.
Ask for the ray of service.
Visualize translucent orange-pink and the number eleven.

Ray Eleven Meditation

Sit or lie in a comfortable position. Close your eyes. Take a few deep breaths and relax.

In your imagination, see yourself at the foot of a very high mountain—one that rises gradually in its elevation. This mountain is shaped like a rounded pyramid or a bell. The top of it seems to disappear into a mist. You are walking on a winding trail that leads to the top of the mountain. It is late afternoon, and the glow of the sun reflects a rainbow of colors as the sun's rays hit the slate color of the mountain. A panorama of exquisite colors makes it appear to you that you are walking up an etheric Rainbow Bridge to the sky.

One color especially catches your eye. It is an indescribable shade of orange-pink; it is not an earthly color, but rather a shade that only God could create. The beauty of this color commands your attention, and you follow it. As you do so, you realize that the knapsack you have been carrying no longer contains the supplies that you originally put in it. It now glows with the same translucent orange-pink and shows you your higher purposes. With each step you take up this rainbow bridge, the sack becomes lighter and you become lighter. You feel yourself merging with the sky, the sun, the Light, the mountain, the bridge. You are all one. There is no separation. There are no boundaries. You feel yourself being bathed in this beautiful Light, and you have become it. Geometric shapes and pastel colors reflect to you a special message of your divine purpose and mission. You finally see who you are, why you are here, and what you are to do in the future. You understand some of the secrets of the universe. You have connected with the whole.

For a brief moment, you look down to see yourself as you were earlier on this mountain path. When you began this trip, you were alone, carrying a heavy load and feeling separate. The mountaintop seemed hopelessly high, and you wondered how you would every climb it. About halfway up the mountain, you saw a Divine Hand reach out and begin to carry you up this path, lightening your load and buoying you up. You watch your previous self expand into this rainbow light and begin to sparkle with divinity. You are amazed to find that the trip is much easier the higher up you go because you are being helped by multitudes of angels and beings of Light. They show you and tell you what you have wanted to know all of your life. What information do they give you? Be with this message for as long as you like. Let the message infuse you. Bathe in its essence.

*You are suddenly aware that you have become part of the Light and you are now helping many lone travelers up the mountain just as you were helped! You are now Unconditional Love and service to all humanity. From this side of the Rainbow Bridge, you see the wholeness of creation. You are amazed at what you could not see on the other side of the Rainbow Bridge. You now understand that merging with the Light for **service** to all is your mission.*

You glow with Unconditional Love. Feel this love for several minutes. Breathe it in, vowing to always keep it in your heart and your mind and your soul—even when you descend the mountain.

It is time to gather up your knapsack and walk back down the mountain to help light the way for those who await you. When you are ready, you may come back in to your physical body. Send a grounding cord in to the center of the Earth, and open your eyes. Smile and radiate the Love of the Creator.

Invoking Ray Twelve

Christ Consciousness

To bring in Ray Twelve, you may use any or all of the following methods, or you can create your own invocation and/or meditation.

Call forth Ray Twelve.

Call forth the golden ray.

Ask for Christ Consciousness.

Imagine the number twelve and visualize gold.

Ray Twelve Meditation

Sit or lie in a comfortable position. Close your eyes. Take a few deep breaths and relax.

Imagine that you have found yourself in a golden city. Everything around you is golden—the streets, the buildings, the trees, all of nature, even the sky is a golden white color. This gold color is so shiny that it is almost mirror-like. Only the people are not gold. They are the normal colors of humans on this planet.

You have found your way to a magnificent golden temple with twelve steps leading to a crystalline golden light within the narrow top of the cathedral. You walk up these steps and come to a landing, where you stop to rest. Inside this landing is a special golden room that beckons you. You enter the room of gold. A flickering golden angel appears and beams special instructions to you. You choose to follow them.

At this moment, you take the most challenging situation in your life and place it in the middle of this golden room. You create a vortex or column of golden Light and bring in the white light of God from an angle. Feel the two beams of light—golden and white—swirling through you and the Earth. This energy raises the vibration of anything that you direct to it in a positive and harmonious way. What situation—personal or planetary—do you direct to it? Take several minutes to see this situation resolved for your highest good and the good of all concerned.

As you watch the transformation of your challenge take place, you become aware of the cosmic purpose of your life and the planet Earth. You see all possibilities, the potential of all life. You understand as never before your connection with the Cosmos and your part in it. What information do you receive? Allow yourself to absorb the essence of this knowledge and great realizations on a vibrational level—to be processed in divine order.

The golden angel of light instructs you that any situation that you place in this golden ray will rise to the surface and clearly show you all of its components. You will rise to the next level and know what to do. The golden ray will help you achieve the Christ Consciousness and see all connected with the Source very clearly. You can bring in the twelfth ray vortex anywhere at any time for any reason. The golden angel gives you twelve golden balls of light to take with you and anchor into your four-body system. Anchor these twelve golden balls of light into the very core of your essence. See these twelve golden balls merge into one golden-white Light within you. Now, see yourself anchoring the golden twelfth ray into your being as your chakras becoming one unified whole. Feel yourself becoming the Christ. You are the Light. You are the Source.

After several minutes of bathing in this glorious golden twelfth ray, it is time to descend the steps of the golden temple and return to Earth. You take the knowledge and realizations of all possibilities with you, forever changed and enlightened. You are empowered with the magic of the twelfth ray to light the way. You will now use this to help lift yourself and humanity higher into the Source. You are transformed and illuminated with golden white light.

When you are ready, slowly come back into your physical body. Send a grounding cord into the center of the Earth, and open your eyes.

Chapter 29

Special Meditations

1—*Healing Meditation*
2—*Meditation to Determine Ray Structures*
3—*Meditation on the Seven Rays*

Healing Meditation

Imagine a shower of golden light coming down from Shamballa. It looks like golden sparkles. See crystalline golden stars showering upon you, cleansing and bathing and healing you of all the debris and negativity of the past. This light is bathing you and elevating you to the height of God. Feel yourself anchor that light into your body.

Bring this energy into your body. Feel its magnificence. It is like a starburst of energy, a sunburst in your heart, radiating out for miles around you. You are the sun. You are the light. See the colors—the rainbow of all the rays—blending and forming a perfect person of light. See yourself beaming in and riding on this twelfth golden ray, your rainbow bridge to the higher dimensions. Feel it lift you into the heart and mind of God. Feel the unconditional love.

Float on a cloud of the color you now see. What color is it that you see? Is it red? Is it orange? Is it yellow? green? blue? indigo? violet? peach? sea-foam green? peach? pearlescence? Meditate for a few moments on each color that you see. How do they make you feel? Feel yourself riding a smooth elevator up through the stars, through all the colors, through the rays. Glide from one color into the next. Feel yourself enveloped by the light. You are a white light, with beautiful prisms of each of the colors, reflecting each of the rays in a beautiful rainbow.

You are in the heart and mind of God. Feel the divine love permeate your entire being. This exquisite love, this magnificent Divine Mother and Divine Father radiates through all of your bodies and heals you. See the golden and the silver and the pink three-fold flame of God anchored in your heart. Feel the healing, bathing, balancing crystalline purity of the light. It is cool light, not hot. Wash away all the negativity, all the fear, all of the imbalance, all that is not of God. See the fear, the negativity, and the imbalance being transmuted now by the perfect, beautiful violet-purple flame. You are enveloped and completely surrounded by the purple fire, the violet flame, which is now transmuting everything that is not desirable, everything that is misqualified or imbalanced within you, into pure divine light substance. Watch it become golden crystalline pyramids of light.

Now see yourself as part of the Divine Plan, receiving sacred knowledge of the Divine Plan. Absorb it into your essence, and let it show you your divine mission and purpose. How truly loved and blessed you are! Know that you are profoundly loved and needed to shine your light upon the earth. God is shining His/Her magnificence into your heart, into your mind, into every cell, into every atom of your being. This light is infusing you with healing energy that uplifts and inspires you. Feel yourself gliding up a staircase through the 352 levels to the highest aspect of God, riding on the Mahatma energy. Archangel Sandalphon is anchoring and integrating this energy into your four lower bodies.

Know that you are a part of all of this, from the center of the Earth to the highest Source. You are all one. You now live vertically, receiving your energy from above rather than from the horizontal exchange of energy with people. You know that the Creator is constantly showering into your essence vital energy and unending love. This vital energy is making you more youthful, radiant, beautiful, and much more alive than ever before. You feel energized... relaxed... blissful...peacefully productive...living in the present time rather than the past.

You have in you the essence of God. You let go of all anxiety, all fear, all feeling of separateness, disconnectedness. You know that you are always one with God.

Feel this bliss for several minutes. When you are ready, gently come back into your body. Send a grounding cord into the center of the Earth. Bring that cord back up through your three lower chakras. When you are ready, open your eyes.

Meditation to Determine Ray Structures

This meditation can be used to assist you in determining the colors in your ray structure or the ray structure of another person.

Close your eyes. Take a few deep breaths, and totally relax your body. Meditate for a few moments on each of the following questions:

> *What is light?*
> *What is vibration?*
> *What is energy?*
> *What are rays?*

After a few moments, affirm inwardly:

> *Life is light.*
> *Life is vibration.*
> *Life is energy.*
> *Life is composed of rays.*

I ask God to show me my rays (or name of person you are doing this meditation for).

I surround myself and (name of person) in a golden dome of divine protection.

Help me (or person you are doing this meditation for) to see our divine missions and rays.

Now, with your eyes still closed, see the colors in the aura of the person you are helping. See the monad at the top, then the soul just below the monad, the personality below that, then the mental body, the emotional body, and the physical body.

What colors do you see?

How do they blend? Are they divided distinctly or do they blend with each other?

Are some of the colors bright and large and others small? Are any of the colors runny and murky? Are the colors clear or muddy?

Scan the aura to see if there is anything polluting those colors.

Find any dark shadows. Identify the shapes, the colors, the muddiness, and the brilliance. In your mind, clean out the darkness or pollution of these colors.

Clean out all polluted areas with the Violet Transmuting Flame and the white Light of God. See the purple/violet flame. See that brilliant White Light of God. If you are willing to do so, send forgiveness to all areas that are polluted. Forgiveness is the key to clearing out every impurity in your colors.

> *Pray for balance.*
> *Pray for peace.*
> *Pray for divine grace.*
> *Thank the Creator for this experience.*

When you are ready, come back into your body. Send a grounding cord from the highest source of God through you to the center of the earth. You may open your eyes when you are ready.

Note: You may want to immediately write down what you experienced. Some people find it helpful to tape-record the session and speak out loud as to what they find in terms of colors, etc.

If you are unable to see any colors or determine any dark shadows or differentiate the colors, do not be discouraged. You will become more skilled as you practice this meditation again and again.

Some people visually "see" colors with their eyes. Others "feel" the colors kinesthetically, and some just "know" what colors they are witnessing. If this does not happen for you, perhaps another method of ray analysis will work better for you.

Meditation on the Seven Rays

The rays build on each other. Their numbered order is highly significant. Ray One **creates with will and power.** *Ray Two builds on Ray One by creating with will, power,* **love and wisdom.** *With Ray Three, you bring in intelligent action with the creation, the will, power, love, and wisdom. You now have* **active intelligence,** *organization and "getting the job done." Ray Four, accordingly, brings in the aspects of* **harmony, beauty,** *and* **art.** *With Ray Five, we add to the creation* **concrete science** *and the scientific manifestation of establishing the Kingdom of God on Earth. Ray Six brings in* **devotion, ideals, religion, and dedication.** *Finally, Ray Seven adds* **"magic" and ceremonial order** *and protocol. When you put all of these together, you have the complete essence of the Creator. The creation is now complete.*

The following meditation can be used at any time to invoke the highest aspects of the Rays. It will help you perfect these qualities in yourself.

Sit or rest in a comfortable position. *Close your eyes and take a few deep breaths. Surround yourself with a golden dome of Divine Protection.* **Affirm inwardly:**

> *I choose today and always to experience the highest aspects of my being.*
> *I ask that the Ascended Masters, Archangels, and great beings of light for each ray assist me in this activity.*
> *I am will and power.*
> *I create with will and power.*
> *I am love.*
> *I am wisdom.*
> *I always create with love.*
> *I always create with wisdom.*
> *I always create with will, power, love, and wisdom.*
> *I am action.*
> *I am active.*
> *I am intelligence.*

I am intelligent.

I am organization.

I am organized.

I create all my deeds and actions with power, love, wisdom, and intelligent, organized action.

I am peace.

I am peaceful.

I am harmony.

I am harmonious.

I am beauty.

I am beautiful.

I am art.

I am artistic.

I bring harmony, beauty, and art into my powerful, loving, wise, and intelligent actions.

I am science.

I am scientific.

I invoke the cosmic scientific manifestation of the kingdom of God on Earth to shine on my powerful, loving, wise, intelligent, harmonious, beautiful, and artistic creations, actions, and deeds.

I am order.

I am orderly.

I am magic.

I am magical.

I am ceremony.

I am ceremonial.

I perform according to protocol.

I am the Violet Flame of Transmutation.

My powerful, loving, wise, intelligent, organized, harmonious, beautiful, artistic, and scientific creations, actions, and deeds are infused with ceremonial order, magic, and protocol.

I invoke the Violet Flame of Transmutation to envelop me and transmute all negativity that comes to me, from me, around me, and within me into pure Divine Light substance.

I am a perfect living embodiment of the perfection of all of the highest aspects of the Seven Rays.

I begin each day with an invocation to have the highest and best experience I can.

I live each day with pure intention, inspiration, and loving purpose.

I go to sleep at night bringing in forgiveness, transmutation, divine protection, and prayer.

I am a beautiful ray of God's Light.

I AM THAT I AM.

Chapter 30

Index of Conditions and Rays

The following is a list of several physical, emotional, mental and spiritual concerns and their corresponding rays. You may use these *rays* and their *colors* to balance and heal these specific areas. Always invoke the highest expression of the corresponding ray to achieve perfect harmony.

Abdomen—Rays One, Two, and Five
Abundance—Rays One and Five
Addictions—Rays Three, Seven and Twelve
Adrenal Glands—Ray Five
Autonomic Nervous System—Ray Six
Bacterial Infections—Ray Four
Balance of Physical Body—Rays One and Four
Bones—Ray Five
Brain—Rays Seven, Eight, Nine, Ten, Eleven and Twelve
Bronchial Tubes—Rays Two, Four and Five
Christ Consciousness—Ray Twelve
Circulation—Rays One and Four
Clarity—Rays Three, Five, Seven and Twelve
Cleansing—Rays Seven and Eight
Communication—Ray Two

Compassion—Ray Two
Control/Manipulation of Others—Rays Three, Seven and Twelve
Cramps—Ray Five
Creativity—Rays Six, Four, Two, Seven and Twelve
Depression—Rays One, Nine and Seven
Digestion—Ray Three
Discretion/Discernment—Ray Two
Emotional Balance—Rays Six, Five and Three
Energy—Rays One and Twelve
Fear—Ray Three
Fever (To Reduce)—Rays Two and Seven
Focus—Rays One, Three, Five and Six
Forgiveness—Rays Two, Four and Seven
Grounding—Ray One
Guilt—Ray Three
Heart—Ray Four
Hormone Production—Ray Three
Hypothalamus—Ray Six
Infections (To Heal)—Rays One, Four and Twelve
Inflammation—Ray Two
Inspiration—Ray Six, Two, Seven and Twelve
Intuition—Ray Six and Twelve
Irritations—Ray Two
Itching—Ray Two
Joy—Ray Nine
Light Body (To Build)—Rays Eight, Nine, Ten, Eleven and Twelve
Liver—Ray Four
Longevity—Rays Four and Twelve
Love—Rays Two and Four
Lungs—Rays Two, Four and Five
Lymphatic System—Ray Three
Manifestation—Ray Five
Motivation—Rays Six and One
Motor and Sensory Nerves—Ray Three

Muscles (To Relax)—Ray Seven
Nervous System—Rays One and Four
Perfectionism—Rays Three and Seven
Personal Power—Rays Three, Two and Seven
Pineal Gland (Stimulation)—Rays Two and Seven
Pituitary Gland—Ray Six
Sedative—Rays Two and Six
Self-Control—Ray Three
Shame—Ray Three
Spleen—Ray Seven
Stimulation of Nervous System and Circulation—Rays One and Four
Stomach—Ray Five
Survival Issues—Ray One
Tact—Ray Three
Thymus Activation—Ray Four
Thyroid—Rays Two and Five
Tolerance—Ray Three
Transmutation/Transformation—Ray Seven
Tumors—Rays Six and Seven
Ultra-Violet Burns—Ray One
Vitality—Rays One and Four
Viruses (To Heal)—Ray Twelve
Well-Being—Rays Two and Four
White Blood Cells—Ray Seven
X-Ray Damage—Ray One

Notes

About the Author

Janet Houser has a Master's Degree in Business Administration and a Bachelor of Science Degree in Education. Her credentials also include extensive study in the fields of numerology, nutrition, soul connections and many healing modalities. She is a certified Jin Shin Jyutsu® practitioner, certified practitioner and teacher of the Melchizedek Method (Levels One, Two, and Three), Life Coach, Spiritual Counselor, teacher of metaphysics, ascension, and self-empowerment classes, college professor, author, speaker, healer, and student of life. She currently lives in Chandler, Arizona.

Janet welcomes your comments, questions and feedback to her book. You may reach her at the email address: *jhouser2@juno.com*, or visit her web site at www.angelfire.com/az3/selfempowered.

Notes

1. Alice A. Bailey, *Discipleship in the New Age*, vol.2, 366.
2. Alice A. Bailey, *A Treatise on the Seven Rays*, in 5 volumes: *Esoteric Psychology*, vol.1, *Esoteric Psychology*, vol. 2, *Esoteric Astrology, Esoteric Healing*, and *The Rays and the Initiations*, Lucis Publishing Company, New York.
3. *Sedona Journal of Emergence*, Light Technology Publishing, Flagstaff, AZ.
4. Ronna Herman, I AM Mastery Course, *STAR*QUEST* 1999, Reno, NV.
5. Ernest Wood, *The Seven Rays* (1925; reprint; Wheaton, IL: Theosophical Publishing House, 1984); 69-71.
6. Ernest Wood, *The Seven Rays* (1925; reprint; Wheaton, IL: Theosophical Publishing House, 1984); 81-100.
7. Alice A. Bailey, *Esoteric Psychology*, vol. I, 210.
8. Zachary F. Lansdowne, *The Rays and Esoteric Psychology* (1989; York Beach, Maine: Samuel Weiser, Inc., 5.
9. Alice A. Bailey, *Esoteric Psychology*, vol. I, 205-207.
10. Zachary F. Lansdowne, *The Rays and Esoteric Psychology*, 5.
11. Alice A. Bailey, *Esoteric Psychology*, vol. I, 202-204.
12. Alice A. Bailey, *Esoteric Psychology*, vol. I, 204-205.
13. Alice A. Bailey, *Esoteric Psychology*, vol. I, 207-208.
14. Alice A. Bailey, *Esoteric Psychology*, vol. I, 208-210.
15. Alice A. Bailey, *Esoteric Psychology*, vol. I, 210-211.
16. Zachary F. Lansdowne, *The Rays and Esoteric Psychology*, 96.

17.Ronna Herman, *I Am Mastery Course, Lesson One*
18.Janet McClure, *Prelude to Ascension,* 170.
19.Ronna Herman, *I Am Mastery Course, Lesson One*
20.Janet McClure, *Prelude to Ascension,* 170.
21.Helen S. Burmester, *The Seven Rays Made Visual,* xv.
22.Alice A. Bailey, *Esoteric Psychology,* **vol. 1, 163.**

Glossary

Archangel Michael—Archangel Michael is in charge of the spiritual enlightenment of all humanity on the Earth. Michael protects our bodies as well as our spiritual destiny and provides us with courage tempered with love and compassion. Archangel Michael is of the First Ray of Divine Will and Power.

Ascension—the achievement of the sixth initiation, where one becomes an Ascended Master; this occurs when the adept and the Light of the Monad merge on the physical pane. The adept's entire being, including the physical body and clothes, is turned into Light; the attainment of the Christ.

Ashram—a recognized group in the consciousness of the illumined initiate, embodying the light of pure reason; the technical name given to the status of those who are on the eve of initiation or who are being prepared for initiation.

Astral Body—the emotions, the emotional body, the level of glamour and emotions.

Chakra—a subtle, spinning wheel of energy or force center within the etheric body.

Christed—infused with the crystal clear Light of the Creator.

Cosmic Ray—referring to the universal or higher ray that affects all in that realm, rather than the personal or individual ray of that entity; for example, our earth is a particular ray, and we are all affected by Ray Three, the ray of our earth. Our Solar System is Ray Two, so we are all affected by Ray Two.

Discipleship—the path which extends from the first to the third initiations; the main lesson of each disciple is learning to express the various aspects of the soul through the mental, emotional, and etheric bodies, resulting in the soul-infused personality.

Emotional Body—the astral body associated with feelings and emotions.

Esoteric Psychology—a psychology that is primarily concerned with the soul; the study of the personality, the soul, and spirit.

Etheric Body—the energy battery of the physical body; the etheric body is an exact replica of the physical body—an archetype upon which the physical form is built. The etheric body is the energy substance a few inches above and around the body. Its function is to store up the rays of radiant light and heat from the sun and to transmit them via the spleen chakra to all parts of the physical body.

Glamour—an emotional reaction that prevents clear perception; the form of delusion on the astral/emotional plane. Glamour is present whenever we have pride, self-pity, or criticism.

Great Central Sun—the Cosmic Source of All That Is; the Source of Life; *not* the sun in the solar system.

Harmonic Convergence—August 15-16, 1987, when the Earth became a fourth-dimensional planet, thus paving the way for the higher galactic rays eight through twelve to be anchored on Earth on January 26, 1991.

Illusion—a false belief or opinion that dominates and distorts thinking; the form of delusion on the mental plane.

Mahatma—means "Father," the highest energy available to the earth, embodying the 352 initiations and levels from Source to Earth.

Metaphysics—the study of the unseen, the invisible forces of life; the study of explaining the reasons behind natural laws.

Monad—the divine spark of God within, the "I AM Presence." The Higher Self of your Higher Self.

Physical Body—the dense physical body plus the physical brain and etheric body.

Ray—a particular quality of energy radiated out from the Creator.

Rays of Aspect—the Three Aspects of the Godhead: Ray One of Divine Will and Power (representing the Father), Ray Two of Love/Wisdom (representing the Son), and Ray Three of Active Intelligence (representing the Holy Spirit).

Rays of Attribute—Rays Four, Five, Six, and Seven are considered auxiliary rays rather than primary rays. These rays are for the purpose of having experiences. After the Third Initiation, people on these rays must blend with the first three major rays.

Second Initiation—achieving mastery over the astral/emotional body.

Self-Mastery—overcoming the lower self: gaining soul and monad control of the personality and physical, emotional, and mental bodies.

Seven Rays—the attributes and characteristics of the Creator that are radiated to our planet from the Source.

Soul Ray—an expression vehicle for spirit; the "higher self" of the body.

Sub-Ray—a ray within a ray. There are seven sub-rays for each ray.

Theosophy—an approach to transform Vedic knowledge and the Eastern mystical teachings into Western thinking; the synthesis of science, religion, and philosophy.

Third Initiation—achieving mastery over the mental body.

Bibliography

Bailey, Alice A. *Discipleship in the New Age,* vol. 1. 1944. Reprint. New York: Lucis Publishing Company, 1976.

_____ . *Discipleship in the New Age,* vol. 2. 1955. Reprint. New York: Lucis Publishing Company, 1972.

_____. *Esoteric Healing.* 1953. Reprint. New York: Lucis Publishing Company, 1977.

_____. *Esoteric Psychology,* vol. 1. 1936. Reprint. New York: Lucis Publishing Company, 1975.

_____. *Esoteric Psychology,* vol. 2. 1942. Reprint. New York: Lucis Publishing Company, 1975.

_____. *Glamour: A World Problem.* 1950. Reprint. New York: Lucis Publishing Company, 1971.

_____. *Initiation: Human and Solar.* 1922. Reprint. New York: Lucis Publishing Company, 1997.

_____. *Letters On Occult Meditation.* 1922. Reprint. New York: Lucis Publishing Company, 1974.

_____. *The Light of the Soul.* 1955. Reprint. New York: Lucis Publishing Company, 1978.

_____. *Ponder on This.* 1971. Reprint. New York: Lucis Publishing Company, 1996.

_____. *The Rays and the Initiations.* 1960. Reprint. New York: Lucis Publishing Company, 1976.

_____. *Serving Humanity.* 1972. Reprint. New York: Lucis Publishing Company, 1999.

_____. *A Treatise on White Magic.* 1934. Reprint. New York: Lucis Publishing Company, 1974.

Besant, Annie. *The Ancient Wisdom.* 1897. Reprint. Adyar, India: Vasanta Press, 1997.

Blavatsky, H. P. *The Secret Doctrine.* 1888. Reprint. Pasadena, CA: Theosophical University Press, 1977.

Burmester, Helen. *The Seven Rays Made Visual.* Marina Del Ray, CA: DeVorss and Company, 1986.

Grattan, Brian. *Mahatma I and II.* Sedona, AZ: Light Technology Publishing, 1994.

Herman, Ronna. *I AM Mastery Course.* Star Quest, 1999.

Lansdowne, Zachary F. *The Chakras and Esoteric Psychology.* York Beach, Maine: Samuel Weiser, 1986.

Lansdowne, Zachary F. *Ray Methods of Healing.* York Beach, Maine: Samuel Weiser, 1993.

_____. *The Rays and Esoteric Psychology.* York Beach, Maine: Samuel Weiser, 1989.

_____. *Rules for Spiritual Initiation.* York Beach, Maine: Samuel Weiser, 1990.

McClure, Janet. *Prelude to Ascension.* Sedona, AZ: Light Technology Publishing 1996.

Stone, Joshua David. *The Complete Ascension Manual*, vol. 1. Sedona, AZ: Light Technology Publishing, 1994.

_____. *Your Ascension Mission.* Sedona, AZ: Light Technology Publishing, 1998.

_____. *Soul Psychology.* Sedona, AZ: Light Technology Publishing, 1994.

Wood, Ernest. *The Seven Rays.* 1925; Reprint: Wheaton, IL; Theosophical Publishing House, 1984.

Printed in the United States
31401LVS00004B/229-252